Foreword

Many histories have been written of   recorded of the Combat Support Ser   Services, whose courage and skill in   such a vital contribution to the moral component of the fighting

This book fills that gap, combining historical fact with anecdotes from those who served.

"207"'s origins pre-date the Territorial Army, but the Manchester Medics have soldiered under the TA banner for over one hundred years.

Having returned from running the "busiest and best trauma hospital in the world" in Afghanistan, it is fitting this book records the achievements of the past as the Volunteers of the present stand ready to meet the challenges of the future.

R G Jackson TD Col
Late Commanding Officer

Colonel R G Jackson, Afghanistan 2010

Figure 2 The Drill Hall on Kings Road, home of the Manchester Medics since 1905. This picture was taken in 1960 when the building was still used as the Manchester Garrison Medical Centre (Courtesy of Manchester Libraries, Information and Archives, Manchester City Council)

The Manchester Medics

PUBLISHED 2014
PRICE £   p

Written and published by Eric Hunter and Lesley Oldham.
Designed and produced by APP Publishing Consultants Ltd, Venture House, Cross Street, Macclesfield, Cheshire SK11 7PG. Tel: 01625 511645 Email: production@app-publishing.co.uk
Whilst the most meticulous care has been taken in the preparation of this publication, the publishers, editors and staff cannot be held responsible for any inaccuracies, errors or omissions, or any consequences arising therefrom, at any time. ISBN 1 898340 03 X

Notes to Reader

The Manchester Medic is a century old story of soldiers, men and women, who have given service to their country whether in time of peace or war. The title, however, is misleading as some of the medics came from Manchester but many were recruited from the towns and villages of Lancashire and more lately Cheshire. What unites them is a building on Kings Road, Old Trafford, Manchester. This HQ, this depot and recruiting centre has remained a permanent feature that unites all the participants in this collective history.

To the avid historian or inquisitive reader an assumption could be made as to where to start trying to discover the unit's history, perhaps records kept by the unit? Unfortunately all records of the origins of the building, Mess minutes and significant events in the unit's history have been lost or destroyed; or rather we could not locate them. Under the guidance of the present Commanding Officer, attempts are now underway to address this and positively project the unit's history as an example to those who may follow.

What the unit does have are the memorials to those who served in the Boer War and those who fell in the Great War. The Rolls of Honours lists their names, each with their own story and unfortunate sad ending. These names became our beginning as they indicated where, when and how the Manchester Medic was involved, in what capacity and in which theatre of war. Individuals were researched and this led us ultimately to their graves, in plots scattered around France and Belgium. We could piece together their history but we could not hear it for ourselves.

The use of narrative, oral or written, forms the basis of the book from the Second World War onwards. We have attempted to give a wide as possible perspective of individuals, rank and gender. We accept that we have a high number of officers; in our defence many started as private soldiers and went up through the ranks. Furthering this eclectic approach we wanted individual stories to provide themes to the history, and explore if these themes held the same measure of consequence from the Second World War to Afghanistan for the individual. Many of these themes did; Annual Camps, training and equipment proved significant to all soldiers, providing good and bad memories. Differences occurred primarily in experiences of training for war and being at war. The history of the unit becomes a collective history shaped externally by world events but internally and personalised by a Manchester Medic at a particular moment. We also realise that certain individuals, Commanding Officers, Matrons and Regimental Sergeant Majors can internally influence the unit with their personality and authority. This history recognises that they needed a considerable team behind them. Subsequently the collective history also acknowledges that a Manchester Medic need not be a medical cap badge but is inclusive of all soldiers who have served with medical units associated with the Kings Road depot. Chefs, drivers, engineers and clerks to name but a few of the occupations that are required to ensure a medical unit functions efficiently, their stories are included.

The history is also ours to tell, we have been selective in what we have included and excluded. The period up to the Second World War was researched with the help of local libraries, the National Archives at Kew and individuals many of them amateur historians. Records of VIP visits have been restricted unless mentioned by a narrative, though lists have been compiled of all 207 Annual Camps and as far as possible of individuals who have mobilised since WW2. The unit does not keep records of those mobilised so we apologise beforehand for any omissions.

All interviews were conducted between 2006 and 2008 and we thank all those who gave up their time and provided us with so many personal accounts. Such has been the interest shown in the project that we continue to receive, written or telephoned information on a weekly basis. There are a lot more stories to be told.

We are acutely aware of gaps in this narrative but researching over a hundred years of history from thousands of participants, it is inevitable that there will be gaps. We believe that the themes identified from the research and the narratives will provide an invaluable insight into the history of the Manchester Medic.

Eric Hunter
Lesley Oldham
September 2014

Acknowledgements

We would like to express our gratitude to all those who have helped in the research and writing of this book. These include the small army of people who spent many hours listening and transcribing the stories and anecdotes from the oral recordings of some of our 'old' and not so 'old' Manchester Medics, and the family and friends of past members who have given us pictures and documents. Our thanks also go to the amateur historians, such as John Hartley and Denis Otter who have allowed us to use their work. The proof readers both military and civilian who we hope have helped make the book accessible by those of a non-military background.

Most of all, we would like to thank all those individuals who have contributed through their oral or written memories to this collective history of our unit.

(Ranks are those given at the time of interview or otherwise indicated during correspondence)

Major David Asher RAMC

Captain Helen Ball QARANC

471333 Major Barry Ford RADC

Warrant Officer Class 2 Jonathan (Jon) Bell RAMC

503706 Lieutenant Colonel John Bennett RAMC

Major Maggie Bremner QARANC

Warrant Officer Class 2 Andrew (Budgie) Burgess RAMC

Staff Sergeant Mark Cecil, RLC (former ACC)

Major Alwyn Charlton RAMC (Field Hygiene Platoon)

Corporal Martin Clarey RAMC (ex RAF)

Mr Michael Coates

454670 Colonel William Elder Late RAMC
(former Commanding Officer 207 General Hospital)

Lieutenant Colonel Marie Farmer QARANC
(12 Casualty Clearing Station, former Matron 207 General Hospital)

Captain Mary Freeman RAMC (former QARANC)

Padre Ian Hall RAChD

Major Colin Gidman RAMC (former RSM 207 General Hospital)

Major Tom Howell RAMC

524195 Captain Malcolm Jackson RAMC

Sergeant Vincent (Vinny) March RAMC

516207 Major Alan McKinnon RAMC

Staff Sergeant Paul Melia RAMC

Staff Sergeant Julie Misell AGC

Sergeant Philip (Phil) Rodgers RAMC

Major Charles Rowland RAMC

24371681 Sergeant Stephen Randall, RLC (former ACC)

Warrant Officer Class 2 Richard (Ricky) Stock RAMC

Major Alan Taberner QARANC (former RAMC)

21043185 Staff Sergeant Tommy Willis RAMC
(126 Field Ambulance, 207 General Hospital)

Dedication

To the men and women of the Territorial Army and their families

In Memory to the following friends and colleagues who passed away during the writing of this book

Colonel William Elder Late RAMC

Lieutenant Colonel Marie Littler (nee Farmer) QARANC

Major Tom Howell RAMC

Corporal Geoff Ashmore

Mr Denis Otter

Table of Contents

Table of Figures	12
Abbreviations	19
Haldane's Army Reforms	23
From Manchester to Mafeking	27
The Great War (1914 – 1918)	38
The TA between the Wars (1919-1939)	55
World War Two (1939-1945)	59
The Cold War	73
First Gulf War 1990-1991, OPERATION (OP) GRANBY	85
People and places	92
TA: Coming from the community	94
Buildings	99
Recruits and Training	102
Training at home and abroad	106
Keeping the Peace	124
Reserve Forces Act 1996	126
The Balkans	127
Second Gulf War and the occupation of Iraq 2003-2009 (OP TELIC)	131
Bastion to Bury	150
The Future	177
The Manchester Medic Post Script	185
Appendix 1 Colonel Sir William Coates	186
Appendix 2 The Eagle	190
Appendix 3 List of Unit members who have served on operations since the end of the Second War	191
OPERATION GRANBY (Gulf War 1) 1990-1991	191
Balkans	192
EXERCISE SAIF SAREEA	193
OPERATION TELIC (2003-2009)	193
Appendix 4 Annual camps of the Manchester Medical units	203
Appendix 5 Additional pictures	206
Bibliography	237
References	238

Table of Figures

Figure 1	Colonel R G Jackson	3
Figure 2	The Drill Hall on Kings Road, home of the Manchester Medics since 1905. This picture was taken in 1960 when the building was still used as the Manchester Garrison Medical Centre (Courtesy of Manchester Libraries, Information and Archives, Manchester City Council)	4
Figure 3	Colonel Sir William Coates (picture taken between 1911 – 12)	22
Figure 4	Illustration of the uniform of a Sergeant, Army Hospital Corps, circa 1878, printed by kind permission of the Wellcome Library, London	29
Figure 5	Captain JW Smith (later Colonel) taken between 1911 and 1914	34
Figure 6	Miss Margaret Elwyn Sparshott, first Matron of 2nd Western General Hospital	36
Figure 7	The Manchester Volunteer Medical Staff Corps (VMSC) in Marching Dress. The gentleman sitting in civilian clothes is thought to be Professor Walter Whitehead who was appointed as Honorary Commandant of the Manchester Companies VMSC in 1900. Picture circa 1900	37
Figure 8	Colonel John Bently Mann and other Staff Officers at the installation of Husain Kamil as the Sultan of Egypt, Sovereign of Nubia, of the Sudan, of Kordofan and Darfur on 20 December 1914	40
Figure 9	Manchester Medics at work in Gallipoli. © Imperial War Museum (Q13316)	41
Figure 10	Lieutenant Colonel H C Parker commanding 1st/1st East Lancashire Field Ambulance dressing the wounds of a Turkish soldier. © Imperial War Museum (Q13258)	42
Figure 11	Private Arthur Gilbert Altham	46

Figure 12	Private Tom Alcock	46
Figure 13	Unloading casualties at 2nd Western General Hospital Headquarters on Whitworth Street	47
Figure 14	Lieutenant Colonel Thomas Holt	49
Figure 15	Private Harry Ingham Hodskinson	53
Figure 16	1st/2nd Field Ambulance taken some time in 1916. The picture includes Harry Hodskinson and other survivors of the Royal Edward	54
Figure 17	1937 winners of the TA Ambulance Challenge Shield held at Millbank London. From left to right Corporal N Ryder, Private G Bradder, Private C Timms and Private H A Cockcroft	58
Figure 18	Bomb damage to the Jewish Hospital (Courtesy of Manchester Libraries, Information and Archives, Manchester City Council)	62
Figure 19	German casualties from Norway being unloaded at 5th (Western) General Hospital (Courtesy of Trafford General Hospital)	62
Figure 20	Bomb damage to Sparshott House, the nurses' recreation hall at Manchester Royal Infirmary, October 1940	62
Figure 21	The RSM and members of the nursing staff of 5th (Western) General Hospital (Courtesy of Trafford General Hospital)	63
Figure 22	Staff Sergeant T Garratt serving lunch in Tobruk. As a Sergeant he was with 125 Field Ambulance when they joined the BEF in 1940. The story of his journey from Europe to Tobruk is not known	68
Figure 23	Pencil drawing showing location of Pantelleria	70
Figure 24	Tom Howell in Italy	70
Figure 25	Warrant Officers' and Sergeants' Mess photographed outside the Kings Road building in 1948	72
Figure 26	Winsor Girls School, Hamm the 'secret' MOBLOC of 207 General Hospital in the event of World War 3 (printed by Kind permission of Kevin Moore ©2012)	73
Figure 27	Stretford detachment drill team on the drill square at Lincoln Barracks, Munster, Germany 1988	75

Figure 28	The Coates room of the Officer's Mess in 1962. From left to right; Colonel J F O'Grady TD, DL (Honorary Colonel 42nd Division 1947-49), Colonel J B Coates MC, Colonel R G W Ollerenshaw TD, QHS (CO 7th General Hospital 1957-60, Colonel J G S Holman MC (CO 7th General Hospital 1963-65), Colonel G A Steele TD, QHP, Colonel R Barraclough MBE, TD, QHS (ADMS 42nd Division 1962-67)	77
Figure 29	WO2 Mark Cecil in his field kitchen	78
Figure 30	Olen, Belgium - 207 General Hospital arriving on Annual Camp, 1976	80
Figure 31	On exercise in Belgium, the ambulance train arriving at the rail head in Olen, 1976	80
Figure 32	In this picture can be seen the then CO, Colonel Elder (on the right) and two future COs; Captain Gallagher (stood with his hands behind his back) and Lieutenant Robertson (sat on the step)	81
Figure 33	Captain Maggie Bremner (left) and two other QARANCs applying a Thomas Splint during the Olen exercise 1976	81
Figure 34	7th (Manchester) General Hospital, Annual Camp, Penhale, Devon 1965	84
Figure 35	Major Paddy Dwyer (front) and Captain Atwal explaining to Prince Philip, Duke of Edinburgh how patients are tracked around the hospital during his visit to the Kings Road Depot in 1999	90
Figure 36	OP GRANBY 1991, aerial photograph of 32 Field Hospital taken from a landing Puma Helicopter	91
Figure 37	Still worn with pride – The Manchester Eagle	94
Figure 38	Colonel J B Coates MC opening Lancaster Detachment	96
Figure 39	Blackburn Detachment at Canterbury Street in the 1990s	98
Figure 40	Members of B Squadron (Blackburn) OP TELIC 4a 2004	98

Figure 41	First Aid training in the Kings Road Drill Hall in the 1960s	100
Figure 42	The Kings Road depot in 1960 at the time it also served as the Manchester Garrison Medical Centre (Courtesy of Manchester Libraries, Information and Archive, Manchester City Council)	101
Figure 43	From left to right, Majors Robert (Bob) Jordon, Colin Gidman and Rodger Sharpe. All ex-regular RSMs of the RAMC	102
Figure 44	Colonel Elder receiving the Lucknow Cup from Major General Hart 1978	104
Figure 45	The Laundry Platoon. These units were independent of the hospital and were cap badged Royal Army Ordnance Corps, Olen, 1976	105
Figure 46	On exercise in Gibraltar 2001	107
Figure 47	Macclesfield Detachment, winners of the 1985 drill competition, Munster. Holding the shield is the then Corporal Charles Rowland	109
Figure 48	NBC training in the 1970s	113
Figure 49	Geoff Ashmore	114
Figure 50	Evacuating casualties during EXERCISE GREEN OCTOPUS, year unknown	117
Figure 51	Colonel Elder with Lieutenant Colonel Mavis Plant (Marton) thought to have been taken at Swynnerton Camp 1976 during EXERCISE GREEN OCTOPUS	117
Figure 52	Manchester Medics on top of Mount Toubkal, Morocco, Armed Forces Day 2009	118
Figure 53	A young Private Steve Randall taken in 1976	119
Figure 54	Manchester Medics winning the female Pegasus competition in 1984	120
Figure 55	Nurses of 12 CCS on Annual Camp, Woowich 1961. Marie Farmer is kneeling on the left of the centre row	121
Figure 56	Manchester Medics in the Ascension Islands 1997	123
Figure 57	Sergeant Martin Clarey on Annual Camp at Penhale in 2011	126

Figure 58   Ilydsa Hospital, Sarajevo. The marks in the wall
            have been caused by small arms fire (2000)   127
Figure 59   Sergeant Vinny March (far right) with other
            members of 207, from left to right,
            Private Darren Smith, Lance Corporals
            Patrick 'Pat' Farrell and David Owen taken on their
            return journey from OP RESOLUTE in 1997   130
Figure 60   Captain Helen Ball, Helen mobilised for OP TELIC
            during the initial war in 2003 and returned the
            following year when she deployed with 207.
            This picture was taken on OP TELIC 4   131
Figure 61   Brotherly love on OP TELIC – SSgt Dave Morgan,
            RE, in DPM temperate (green), who served with
            202 (Midlands) Field Hospital and Sgt Phil Morgan,
            RE, in DPM desert, who served with 16 Close
            Support Medical Regiment   135
Figure 62   OP VERITY 2003, sitting on the right is
            Captain Mary Freeman keeping the senior
            nursing staff up to date with progress   136
Figure 63   Hospital on Parade, final preparations in York
            before departing for OPTAG at Lydd. The squad
            to the left of the picture are the logistical section
            made up mainly of 152 (Ulster) Transport Regiment 137
Figure 64   Winding down after a day's training at Lydd.
            The Second in Command, Lieutenant Colonel
            Mike Godkin (with ball) next to him, with his back
            to the camera, is the then Corporal Martin Clarey   138
Figure 65   Captain Sharon Wright checking and sending last
            minute messages before flying out of Brize Norton   138
Figure 66   Sun rise over MND (SE) Field Hospital, A&E   140
Figure 67   Sun rise over MND (SE) Field Hospital, wards   140
Figure 68   Major Alan Taberner showing his softer side
            – or is it lunch!!   141
Figure 69   WO2 Ricky Stock RAMC   143
Figure 70   WO2 Jon Bell carrying one of our young casualties
            back to ITU after surgery   144
Figure 71   On the right is Colonel Godby (the outgoing CO),
            on the left Colonel Bhatnagaer (the incoming CO)   144

Figure 72	Captain Malcolm Jackson	147
Figure 73	Major Sharon "Queen of the Mops" Stewart	147
Figure 74	Major Val Johnson (front row, sitting wearing dark brown t-shirts) with members of her theatre staff, both UK and Czech	147
Figure 75	Tommy Willis shares a cheeky joke with Corporal Steve Booth and the newest member of 207 to deploy, Private Chrissy Barwick	157
Figure 76	The hospital simulator at AMSTC, 207 conducting their MSE prior to deployment. In the foreground with his back to the camera is Major Steve Hawes [Crown Copyright/MOD 2010]	158
Figure 77	Pictured in the Emergency Department (ED) at Bastion, Major Steve Hawes with his American Navy counterpart Captain Ed Turner	160
Figure 78	Corporal David Sykes sat at one of the CT scanner terminals	162
Figure 79	The blood donor panel in action, Majors Rosalind (Ros) Peel (right) and Angie Nicholls (left), on the bed Captain Beth Hall Thompson one of the General Duties Medical Officers. This was probably one of the few times Beth was able to 'put her feet up' during her tour of duty.	164
Figure 80	Taken outside the hospital entrance, Staff Sergeant Paul Melia (right), Major Simon Davies (Centre) and the RSM of 16 Medical Regiment	167
Figure 81	Staff Sergeant Julie Misell with one of the regular visitors to the hospital. Military working dogs would attend the hospital both to visit patients and as patients themselves	168
Figure 82	Padre Ian Hall (left) and Padre Andy Earl taken outside the Hospital Chapel St Luke's	171
Figure 83	Penny (left) and Jayne with Captain Michael Hughes and Staff Sergeant Andrew Higgins (right)	172
Figure 84	Corporal David Sykes with the HMC Father Christmas (Corporal Scott Jibson)	173

Figure 85	The Hospital Christmas Eve Carole Concert. In the centre Colonel Robin Jackson. To his left Private Chrissy Barwick and other members of the nursing staff	**173**
Figure 86	Letter addressed to all hospital personnel on the last day of 207 (Manchester) Field Hospital's tour	**175**
Figure 87	207 (Manchester) Field Hospital's home coming parade, Bury, March 2011	**176**
Figure 88	Manchester Eagle	**183**
Figure 89	207 (Manchester) Field Hospital Freedom of the City of Manchester	**184**
Figure 90	The Manchester Eagle	**190**
Figure 91	Extract from a letter sent by Colonel Robert Ollerenshaw to the War Office 20 Jan 1959 (source WO32/18854, The National Archives)	**190**

Abbreviations

2IC	Second in Command
ADMS	Assistant Director Medical Services
ADS	Advance Dressing Station
AELO	Air Evacuation Liaison Officer
AGC(SPS)	Adjutant General's Corps (Staff & Personnel Support)
AHC	Army Hospital Corps
AMO	Administrative Medical Officer
AMS	Army Medical Services
AMSTC	Army Medical Services Training Centre
ANZAC	Australian and New Zealand Army Corps
AOR	Area of Operations
BEF	British Expeditionary Force
CBRN	Chemical, Biological, Radiological and Nuclear
CCAST	Critical Care Air Support Team
CSMR	Close Support Medical Regiment
CSS	Casualty Clearing Station
CMT	Combat Medical Technician
CO	Commanding Officer
ED	Emergency Department
EFI	Expedition Forces Institutes
ELFA	East Lancashire Field Ambulance
FMHT	Field Mental Health Team
HMC	Hospital Management Cell
HQ	Headquarters
ICU	Intensive Care Unit
IRA	Irish Republican Army

MA	Medical Assistant
MERT	Medical Emergency Response Team
MFT	Medical Treatment Facility
MND(SE)	Multi National Division (South East)
MO	Medical Officer
MOBLOC	Mobilisation Location
MRI	Manchester Royal Infirmary
MT	Motor Transport
NAAFI	Navy, Army, Air Force Institutes
NATO	North Atlantic Treaty Organisation
NBC	Nuclear, Biological, Chemical
NCO	Non Commissioned Officer
OC	Officer Commanding
OP	Operation
OPTAG	Operational Training and Advisory Group
PIRA	Provisional Irish Republican Army
PSI	Permanent Staff Instructor
PT	Physical Training
QAIMNS	Queen Alexandra's Imperial Military Nursing Service
QARANC	Queen Alexandra's Royal Army Nursing Corps
QM	Quarter Master
RAChD	Royal Army Chaplains' Department
RADC	Royal Army Dental Corp
RAMC	Royal Army Medical Corps
RASC	Royal Army Service Corps
RCT	Royal Corps of Transport
RE	Royal Engineers

RHQ	Regimental Headquarters
RiP	Relief in Place
RLC(V)	Royal Logistical Corps (Volunteers)
ROSO	Regimental Operational Support Officer
RPG	Rocket Propelled Grenade
RQMS	Regimental Quarter Master Sergeant
RSOI	Reception Staging and Onward Integration
RSM	Regimental Sergeant Major
SLB	Shaibah Logistics Base
SNCO	Senior Non Commissioned Officer
SO	Staff Officer
TA	Territorial Army
TAVRA	Territorial Army and Volunteer Reserve Association
TD	Territorial Decoration
TF	Territorial Force
TFNS	Territorial Force Nursing Service
TNC	Trauma Nurse Coordinator
UK	United Kingdom
UOR	Urgent Operational Requirement
VAD	Voluntary Aid Detachment
VMSC	Volunteer Medical Staff Corps
WO1	Warrant Officer Class 1
WO2	Warrant Officer Class 2
WW2	World War 2

Figure 3 Colonel Sir William Coates (picture taken between 1911 – 12)

Haldane's Army Reforms

'No Army is worth anything which is not ready to take the field'
Lord Richard Burdon Haldane

Within the ranks of the Liberal Government formed in 1905 were some of the men who would dominate British politics up to the start of the Great War and beyond. They included: David Lloyd George, Winston Churchill and Herbert Asquith. It would be the last Liberal Government the country would have, but it would lay down the foundations of many of the institutions we know today, such as old age pensions and a system of insurance against unemployment and sickness. It also undertook to reform the Army and in doing so created the Territorial Army (then the Territorial Force).

Mr Richard Burdon Haldane (later Lord Haldane) was appointed Secretary of State for War in December 1905, taking over a department whose expenditure was spiralling out of control. In ten years the Army's expenditure had risen from £18 million to nearly £30 million and personnel levels had grown by nearly 50,000. Despite all this expenditure repeated attempts to reform the Army had failed. This was clearly demonstrated by the Boer War (1899 – 1902) which had cost £210 million and the loss of over 20,000 men, to defeat, in the words of H G Wells, 'a handful of farmers'. [1, 2]

The Boer War was a wake-up call for the British nation. She was still at the height of her industrial and imperial powers. A few 'farmers' should not have posed much of a problem, however in just one week in December 1899, the Boers were to inflict three defeats on British Forces, leaving a shocked nation with the realisation that their 'invincible' Army was not quite as invincible as they had thought. It was to take the Imperial Forces three years to overcome the Dutch Afrikaners and was to demonstrate, and not for the first time, the organisational and administrative problems within the British Army. With these events still fresh in the mind, the Esher Committee of 1904 made several recommendations with regard to the Army that would lay the foundations for Haldane's later reforms: [3]

The abolition of the Commander-in-Chief of the Forces, to be replaced by the General Staff

The creation of an Army Council whose members would include the War Ministers and the four members of the newly created General Staff

The centre for defence planning should be the Committee of Imperial Defence

Several factors played a part in Haldane's decision making before he presented his Bill to Parliament: he wanted to provide a British Expeditionary Force (BEF) that was capable of deploying to any trouble spots. This had its own problems: in the early 1900s war on mainland Europe was just one possibility. The Empire was vast and the BEF needed to be able to respond quickly to any threat to British Dominions. It would also be required to maintain itself in the field for several months, since resupply and communication could pose a problem if the force was deployed to far-flung corners of the Empire. Another problem was man power: In 1907 Haldane doubted it would be possible to mobilise 100,000 troops and indeed that this figure was optimistic. There was a need to provide a pool of replacements that could be drafted at short notice to fill gaps in the Regular Army on mobilisation and supply reserves to replace men lost during any war. The Boer War had also highlighted the need for better training. If the Army could not easily defeat a few 'farmers', how would it cope when faced with a professional well-trained Army? Once the BEF deployed, who would defend the Homeland? [4]

Haldane had two other considerations that are as relevant today as they were then; finance and politics. The Liberal Government was intent on social reforms and needed the funds to carry them out, so Haldane had to provide the country with an Army that was efficient whilst at the same time reduce its cost to the nation. It should be noted that several of his predecessors had failed in their attempts to reform the Army because of intense political opposition. [5]

In February 1907 Haldane addressed Parliament [4] and laid out his plans for the reform of the Army[1]. It had been decided to form the Army into divisions rather than Army Corps, since it was easier to

---
1   The Haldane reforms focused on the organisation of the Army within the British Isles and did not deal with the battalions stationed abroad.

contract or expand a division than an Army. The new home-based Army would consist of two lines with 'bridges' between the lines.

The first line would consist of six divisions and four cavalry brigades; these would form the Regular Army and be held in such a state of readiness that in the event of war they could mobilise and maintain themselves in the field for up to six months. The second line would be created from the existing Auxiliary Forces; the Militia, the Yeomanry and the Volunteers. This new Territorial Force (TF) would mirror the Regular Army and be organised on divisional lines and for the first time funding would be provided centrally by the War Office. Britain was already divided into twelve Regimental Districts, these would be reorganised to form fourteen divisions consisting of forty-two infantry brigades with cavalry, artillery and divisional support elements. The infantry would come from the ranks of the Militia, the Cavalry from the Yeomanry and the Artillery and non-combatants (for example medical, engineering) from the Volunteers.

In order to provide the Regular Army with an adequate number of drafts quickly during a time of mobilisation, Haldane increased the number of "A" reservists and created the Special Reserves who were paid a yearly bonus that made them eligible for service overseas. The "A" reserves were a group of men who, upon retirement from the Regular Army could be recalled for service. The Special Reserve was formed from the old Militia (who did not wish to become part of the new TF) and men of the new TF who were willing to serve overseas. The need for the TF to volunteer for overseas service as part of the Special Reserve was particularity important when it came to the non-combatant element of the second line, since these would provide the Regular Army, at a time of mobilisation, with the extra medical and logistical support not normally required during peace time.

In order to train the Reserves, new training battalions would be established around the country and an Officer Training Corps was to be created.

The terms of engagement for TF would be an enlistment period of four years with the option to leave after giving three months' notice. In the event of war they could be called up for six months training but could not be compulsorily sent overseas[2]. The duties of the TF were to garrison the naval ports and to take the place of Regular troops in the event of full scale mobilisation of the Regular Army and Regular Reserves. They would also act as a home defence force should the country be invaded.

To administer the new force each county would have its own Association (the fore runner of the Reserve Forces and Cadets Associations) to be presided over by the Lord-Lieutenant and would have responsibility for the units that lay within their boundaries. These associations would relieve the unit Commanding Officer of the burden of raising funds and supplies and free him to concentrate on commanding and training. The associations would also act as a bridge between the Commanding Officers of the TF and the Regular Army.

The Territorial and Reserve Forces Act 1907 was successfully passed by Parliament and on 1 April 1908 the new Territorial Force came in to existence.

Haldane made several compromises to the Bill in order to ease its passage thought Parliament. One was the concession that the TF could not be compulsorily called up for service overseas. It was one of the terms of service that was fiercely protected by members of the Volunteers when the Territorial Army (TA) was reformed in 1921. It has been used by critics of the TF/TA since it came in to existence – "what use is an Army that cannot be compulsorily mobilised for service where needed whether home or abroad".

Haldane's Army estimate for 1907-08 forecast a saving of £2.6 million bringing expenditure below £28 million to the delight of the Liberal Party [5]. He also created an environment that would lead to the professional British Army that we know today, and a military force that would become respected throughout the world.

---

[2] Haldane assumed that at a time of national crisis the TF would volunteer for service abroad, he was to be proven right on the outbreak of the Great War in 1914.

From Manchester to Mafeking

Until the introduction of the Territorial Force Scheme, the Volunteers were a splendid body from one point of view. They were a mass of enthusiastic individuals and units with, in many cases, a large number of efficient officers and men, but without any organisation or comprehension of future requirements. [6]
page 272
Colonel Sir William Coates

The 'volunteer' in military terms is nothing new. For centuries, when the country was in danger of invasion, men with little or no military experience would 'step up to the line' and take up arms, ready to defend their homes and communities. When the danger passed these volunteers would disappear in to the ether as quickly as they had formed. A notable exception is The Honourable Artillery Company (the Guild of St George), a militia that was granted its Charter of Incorporation by King Henry VIII in 1537 and is now the second most senior unit of the TA [7].

Throughout the 1800s, the threat of invasion was a constant fear and with the assassination attempt on Napoleon III this threat became real. In 1858, Volunteer Corps were raised up and down the country. Unlike the previous incarnations these Volunteers did not disappear and it was out of these Corps that the volunteer medical services eventually evolved.

Only four years previously, Britain, then allied with France, had engaged in a war that would highlight not only the ineptitude of the British Army at that time but the inadequacies of its military medical services.

The Crimean War (1854 – 1856) is perhaps best remembered for Florence Nightingale and the Charge of the Light Bridge, it was also possibly the first case of embedded journalism. The newly invented telegraph allowed the first War Correspondents such as William Russell, to report events within days of their happening in the British press. The plight of wounded British soldiers and the conditions in which they were treated were widely reported, and it is a sad reflection on medical facilities of the time, that out of the 22,000 British deaths during the war only 4,000 were battle casualties[3] [8, 9]. Surgeon Lieutenant Colonel George Evatt describes in 1894 why he believed the medical services failed.

> Both places[4] failed because the Medical Services of 1854 was a weakly organised, subdivided corps, without authority, without any trained staff of subordinates, and quite ignorant of the needs and demands of how to clear a battlefield of wounded and how to organise a hospital to treat 4,000 sick at one time. [10] page 219

At the time the Army Medical Department was a civilian part of the War Office and Medical Officers had no power to influence their regimental commanders. They had no trained medical orderlies, except for those they trained themselves and each regiment would provide a hospital for the care of its own men. Thus a wounded soldier would be sent to his regimental hospital, and not necessarily the site of best medical care for his injuries. There was also no organised plan of evacuation for the wounded and with little or no dedicated transport, reaching the Base Hospital was haphazard at best. [10-12]

The low regard that the combat arms held for the medical services was demonstrated by Lord Raglan, Commander-in-Chief of British Forces, who, wishing to create a mobile force, ordered that regiments would take to the field without any hospital equipment and only limited medical supplies. [12]

When the newly formed Ambulance Corps arrived in the Crimean 1854 the Times reported:

> "...they have been found in practice rather to require nurses themselves than to be able to nurse others. At Gallipoli and in Bulgaria they died in numbers, while the whole of them were so weak as to be unable to perform the most ordinary duties..." [9] page 192.

In 1855 a second attempt was made to form a hospital corps but the Medical Staff Corps fared little better than the Ambulance Corps and in 1857 the Army Hospital Corps (AHC) was formed. Unlike their predecessors the ranks of this Corps were recruited from the line regiments and had, not only to be of good conduct, but were also

---

3   This reflects the standard of medical care in general at the time, both military and civilian. The Cholera epidemic of 1854 claimed 20,000 lives in Britain.

4   He is talking of Alma and the Base Hospital at Constantinople, Scutari

required to be able to read and write (not a common attribute amongst the rank and file of that time). The AHC would have a formal rank structure and its own officers however these were drawn from the combat arms not the medical services. It would be many years before Medical Officers would gain command of the men who worked for them. [12]

The Army Medical Services (AMS) continued to develop along two different lines. The Medical Staff, made up of the qualified doctors and surgeons, and the AHC consisting of other ranks trained as orderlies, stewards, cooks and storekeepers. In 1884 under reorganisation the AHC name reverted back to the Medical Staff Corps. These two lines were eventually combined in to one Corps on 23 June 1898, when under a Royal Warrant, the Royal Army Medical Corps came in to existence. [12]

Whilst the Regular AMS fought to improve and develop itself, a volunteer medical service did not exist except for the presence of the volunteer Regimental Medical Officer. These Medical Officers were recruited by individual volunteer units and there was no equivalent of the Medical Staff Corps within the volunteer movement. It was not until the 1880s that the seeds of the volunteer medical movement were sown.

Figure 4 Illustration of the uniform of a Sergeant, Army Hospital Corps, circa 1878, printed by kind permission of the Wellcome Library, London

Surgeon Major Peter Sheppard was in the process of writing a book on "First Aid to the Injured" when he was unfortunately killed during the Zulu War. His manuscript found its way in to the hands of a Mr James Cantlie, a Senior Assistant Surgeon at Charing Cross Hospital. Cantlie began to give lectures on First Aid and it was at one of these lectures that he met Sergeant Maclure of the London Scottish Volunteers who was an instructor in stretcher drills. Maclure realised the importance of teaching First Aid and stretcher drills to the Volunteers, and Cantlie saw benefits in doing the same with medical students. Cantlie invited medical students at Charing Cross to train in stretcher drills and 72 took up the offer. His vision was that, upon qualifying, these young surgeons would disperse up and down the country, join Volunteer regiments as Medical Officers and be able to instruct the volunteers in stretcher drills and First Aid. It also went a step further; [12, 13]

> ....*I believed also I saw a connecting link whereby the surgeons might be gathered together into a coherent body instead of existing as separate units; the genesis in fact of the Volunteer Medical Association[5]. [13] page 33*

Sir James Cantlie

Cantlie was supported in his endeavour by a Regular Army Surgeon by the name of George Evatt. Surgeon Major Evatt had joined the Army Medical Department in 1865 and had seen service in various parts of the Empire. He was not only a great advocate of reform within the Army Medical Department but also a great supporter of the volunteer medical movement and the employment of female nurses within the military (the majority of the Army at this time being against the presence of women within its ranks). In 1884 Evatt accompanied Cantlie on a tour of universities to promote the idea of the Volunteer Medical Association, and new companies were formed in Edinburgh, Manchester, Leeds, Woolwich, Maidstone and Dublin. On 1 April 1885 the hard work of Colonel James Cantlie and Surgeon Major Evatt resulted in the Volunteer Medical Staff Corps (VMSC) being gazetted with the constitution of four companies in the City of London. [12]

Whilst addressing a meeting at Owens College in Manchester, Colonel Cantlie and Surgeon Major Evatt came into contact with a young doctor who was already an acting surgeon with the 20th Lancashire Rifle Volunteers[6]; his name was William Coates (Appendix 1). Coates had moved to Manchester, after completing his medical training in London, to begin a medical practice in Moss Side. He would continue to practice medicine well into his 90s and lived in Manchester until his

---

5   The Volunteer Medical Association would eventually become the Volunteer Medical Staff Corps.
6   This unit became the 8th (Ardwick) Battalion (TF), The Manchester Regiment and served in both the First and Second World War.

death in 1962 at the age of 101. He was instrumental in the development of volunteer medical services, not just in Manchester but throughout the country. He was a member of Lord Haldane's committee in 1906 – 07 on the formation of the TF; he was appointed Assistant Director Medical Services (ADMS) Western Command and assisted in the formation and control of all hospitals in that command during the First World War. His involvement in volunteer medical services was not restricted to the military. In 1910 he formed the British Red Cross Society in East Lancashire and during the First World War helped to form the Totally Disabled Soldiers Home at Broughton House, Salford and two other homes: Wyborne Gate[7] in Southport and one in Blackburn. He was still active during the Second World War, slightly offended that his medical skills had not been called upon (although now aged 79). He did however get involved with the administration of pensions[8] (possibly army pensioners). But all this was yet to come; for now, this young Acting Surgeon would content himself with the formation of the Manchester Volunteer Medical Staff Corps. [6, 14]

The volunteer of 1885 was totally different from the so called 'volunteer' of today. For a start the volunteer paid to join by means of an annual subscription and there was no central funding. In order to be recognised by the War Office as a division[9] of the VMSC, the Manchester Medics would be required to enrol 100 officers and men, clothe and equip them and provide a location for training and administration, as Coates himself describes:

> .... *Men were enrolled, chiefly medical and other students at first, rules were drafted by which each man had to pay 10s. 6d. a year subscription and a £1 towards the cost of his uniform. We collected about £100 also from the medical officers of other units, and obtained altogether some £500 at this time, with which uniforms were bought and a house, 98, Burlington Street, rented, and equipment such as stretchers, haversacks, bandages, etc., purchased...[6] page 273.*

---

7   In total four houses were purchased for use as homes for disabled service men. The fourth Grangethorpe became an orthopaedic hospital. Broughton House still exists and continues to care for ex service personnel both male and female.
8   Recollections of Sir William Coates during World War Two by his grandson Michael, interview at Sir William Coates House, Kings Road Stretford 2007.
9   Division here does not denote an Army Division but describes a distinct group of a larger organisation

The Drill Hall of the 16th Lancashire Rifle Volunteers was also located on Burlington Street. Their Commanding Officer, Lord Ellesmere, allowed the Medics to use it for drill, with the rented house being used for training and administration. On 1 April 1887 the Manchester Medics were taken over by the War Office as the 4th Division, Volunteer Medical Staff Corps strength 101. [6]

In the late Victorian age, the volunteer would engage in many of the activities that TA soldiers would recognise today: attend Annual Camp and go away for periods of two days training, with the difference once again that the volunteer paid for the privilege.

The company did not go to camp in 1887 but I organised a two-day route march (June 3 and 4, 1887) at Worksop in full dress.... Numbering two officers (Rayner and myself) and thirty-five other ranks, we marched twenty-five miles in the pouring rain the first day, after parading outside the old Manchester Royal Infirmary at 5a.m. and entraining for Worksop.... On the Second night we reached Worksop just in time to catch a train which arrived in Manchester at 11.30p.m., the company dismissed again outside the old Infirmary. Each member paid his own fare and 6s. 6d. towards expenses. I still have a note that it cost me £4 5s. 11d.! [6] page 274

Colonel Sir William Coates

The volunteers at this time were military clubs frequented in the main by the middle class. They were almost entirely self-funding, with the officers of each of the Volunteer Companies being personally liable for any funding short falls. In 1898 when the Manchester Medics were in danger of losing the use of their Headquarters (now at 336 Chester Road) Coates bought the house and rented it back to the Corps. When this building became too small to house the ever expanding 4th Division VMSC, Coates was left with a house and no tenant. As the 19th century gave way to the 20th the volunteers gradually changed; more working class men joined and funding began to filter down from government grants. The volunteers had been raised for Home Defence, but by the start of the 20th Century their ability to fulfil such a task had been called into question. The Boer War brought even more criticism when only 13,000 out of a volunteer force of 230,000, volunteered for overseas service [5, 6].

...One of the things I remember him saying was that we started with just a Platoon and then we got a Company, in fact at the time of the Boer War we got a Division...
Michael Coates talking about his grandfather William Coates

Surgeon Captain William Coates was gazetted to command the 4th Division VMSC in December 1897, and on 23 June[10] the following year the Royal Army Medical Corps (RAMC) received its Royal Warrant. The volunteers were accorded the same privileges as their Regular RAMC counterparts and officers of the new corps were granted substantive rank, with the prefix "Surgeon" being removed from the Medical Officer title. The Manchester Companies of VMSC enjoyed a healthy existence, having two fully recruited companies and a waiting list. Repeated requests to create new companies were turned down by the War Office [6]. This happy peaceful existence was about to be shattered by the Boer War. This would be the first time the Manchester Medics would be tested and they would not be found wanting.

From the Crimean War up to the start of the Boer War, improvements in medical care had been slow due partly to the lack of funding from the War Office and partly to the indifference shown by the combat arms to the role of the medical services. Changes had been made in the organisation of the Army Medical Services: regimental appointments had, for the most part, been abolished as had Regimental Hospitals and thought had been given to a chain of evacuation [10]. However recruitment into the Army Medical Services had been poor and at the start of the war only 850 Medical Officers and ten hospitals were sent to South Africa to support the Army. The lack of medical staff and the lack of understanding by the combat arms of the importance of hygiene and sanitation meant that once again it would be disease and not battle that would claim the majority of lives, with typhoid alone killing 13,000 in comparison to the 8,000 killed in battle [8].

---

10 Each year the RAMC celebrate 'Corps Day' on 23 June

On 5 February 1900 the War Office asked if the Manchester Companies of the VMSC could supply a bearer company for service in South Africa. Only seven days later, on 13 February Captain JW Smith with four officers and 106 other ranks left Manchester for Aldershot on route to South Africa. From then until the end of the war, Chester Road became a recruiting Depot. [6]

The request to form new companies that the War Office had for so long rejected was now authorised, and by June 1902 the Manchester Companies VMSC expanded from two to seven companies. An eighth company was raised in Bolton in March 1905. The Manchester Medics had become the largest organisation of its kind in the country. Little is known about where and what the Manchester Medics did during the War. It is known that Captain Smith served for some months at the No. 9 General Hospital at Bloemfontein and that a number of men joined No. 5 General Hospital, but the rest were dispersed upon or shortly after arrival in Africa. On their return many of the men were unhappy that the company had been split up and they had lost their unit identity as a result of this, several years later, when asked to form part of the Special Reserve[11] the Manchester Companies refused to join[12]. [6, 15]

Figure 5 Captain JW Smith (later Colonel) taken between 1911 and 1914

By the end of the Boer War the Manchester Companies VMSC were so large that 336 Chester Road was no longer adequate for their needs, and with little room for development on the site, a new location was sought for a new Drill Hall and headquarters. On 18 January 1905 General Sir Henry Mackinnon formally opened the new headquarters on Kings Road. Since that time the building has been continually occupied by various aspects of the Army Medical Services and is today the home of 207 (Manchester) Field Hospital (Volunteers). [6]

---

11 As part of the Special Reserve, the men would have been compelled to serve overseas.
12 When 18 Special Reserve Field Ambulance was formed in Manchester in 1908, men of the Manchester Companies VMSC only agreed to join after Coates received assurances from the War Office that they would be deployed as a complete unit.

The Manchester Medics welcomed many famous visitors to their new building such as Sir Alfred Keogh and Sir Frederick Treves. In November of 1907 during his tour of the country to promote his ideas for the TF Mr Haldane came to the new Drill Hall to address the companies of the VMSC. The following year, at the birth of the TF, the Manchester Companies of the VMSC were replaced by three Field Ambulances and a General Hospital of the Royal Army Medical Corps (Territorial Force).

The East Lancashire Divisional Medical establishment was [6]:

Divisional Headquarters: Administrative Medical Officer (AMO)
1 Staff Officer to AMO
1 Sanitary Officer
6 Other Ranks

Field ambulances: 1st East Lancashire Field Ambulance
10 Officers
263 Other Ranks
1 Permanent Staff

2nd East Lancashire Field Ambulance
10 Officers
247 Other Ranks
2 Permanent Staff

3rd Field Ambulance
10 Officers
252 Other Ranks
1 Permanent Staff

General Hospital (2nd Western): 3 Officers
43 Other Ranks
24 *a la suite*[13] medical officers

RAMC TF Training School: 1 Officer (who also acted as the Adjutant)
1 Permanent Staff

---

13 The *a la suite* medical staff of the hospital were made up of specialist consultants who could be called upon when the Hospital was mobilised.

For the first time the Manchester Medics would welcome females in to their ranks, if only in an honorary capacity. Miss Margaret Elwyn Sparshott became the first Principal Matron of 2nd Western General Hospital on the formation of the TF. She had arrived in Manchester to take up the post of Lady Superintendent of Nurses at the Manchester Royal Infirmary in 1907 and held both appointments until her retirement in 1929. [16]

Figure 6 Miss Margaret Elwyn Sparshott, first Matron of 2nd Western General Hospital

By 1908 the Manchester Medics had grown from that small meeting of students at Owens College to a medical organisation capable of supporting the East Lancashire Division (TF). In 1910, the medics attended their first Divisional Camp after the formation of the TF, on Salisbury Plain. Here they encountered the Commander-in-Chief of the Southern Command who had this to say of the Manchester Medics:

The most complete and best turned-out units that Lancashire has sent to Salisbury Plain are the three field ambulances of the RAMC East Lancashire Division TF.

The men are a fine lot, drawn from a superior class; they know their drill and move splendidly, added to which the three field ambulances are right up to establishment and have pretty nearly every man in camp for a full fortnight [6] page 338

General Sir Ian Hamilton

They would encounter General Hamilton again under quite different circumstances in 1915.

Figure 7 The Manchester Volunteer Medical Staff Corps (VMSC) in Marching Dress. The gentleman sitting in civilian clothes is thought to be Professor Walter Whitehead who was appointed as Honorary Commandant of the Manchester Companies VMSC in 1900. Picture circa 1900

The Great War (1914 – 1918)

While the Proclamation announcements were yet wet upon the walls, we set our faces in the direction of the Depot in Old Trafford. The men in no unit in the East Lancashire Territorial's obeyed the calling-up summons with greater alacrity than we.
[17] page 1
Sergeant A E F Francis 2/3rd East Lancashire Field Ambulance

At the outbreak of the Great War it looked at first as if Haldane would return to the War Office; he was now the Lord Chancellor and Asquith (the Prime Minister) had it in mind that he and Haldane would run the War Office together. There was wide mistrust of Haldane who was thought to have German sympathies. The job instead went to Field Marshal Earl Kitchener of Khartoum, a great hero of the British people, who happened to be in Britain on leave prior to the outbreak of the Great War in August 1914. His appointment was greeted with almost universal approval by the general public, if not by the politicians. [18]

Haldane's reforms of 1908 had set in place a mechanism by which, in the event of war, the Regular Army could deploy at once, with the TF being mobilised to undergo six months training before being asked to volunteer for overseas service. The County Associations would be responsible for the recruitment of new men for the Army. Kitchener refused to use Haldane's system; instead he would create a new army, recruited via the Regular Army system of recruitment [5, 18]. This new army would consist of service battalions that would later become better known as the Pals battalions.

Kitchener had many reasons for not using Haldane's system. He had worked with volunteers on several occasions, including the Boer War, and had a low opinion of their capability. The TF itself probably only reinforced Kitchener's view by the slow response to the call to volunteer for Imperial Service overseas at the start of the war. He had served abroad for most of his life and was unaware of how Haldane's reforms had increased the efficiency of the TF. Kitchener was also one of the few people who predicted that the war would last for at least three years and he felt that the existing military system would be unable to cope with the number of recruits required to maintain the army in the field for this time. [5, 18]

Views on Kitchener's treatment of the TF vary, but by the end of the War the TF felt badly let down, not only by its perceived ill treatment by Kitchener, but also by the War Office in general. This would have repercussions after the war when the TF was being reformed [5].

Kitchener may have wanted to create 'New Armies' but it would take time to train them, and he needed troops for the Western Front. Despite his misgivings he would have to make use of the TF and in early August 1914 Kitchener let it be known that if any TF unit offered to volunteer for Imperial Service abroad it would be accepted [5, 18]. The response to the call to take up Imperial Service may have been mixed around the country, but in East Lancashire it was decisive. Within a few days of Kitchener's call for volunteers for overseas service, 90% of the officers and men of the East Lancashire Division had signed for imperial overseas service [19]. Less than a month later, as the Regular Army's BEF deployed for service in France and Belgium, the East Lancashire Division sailed for Egypt. Now titled 42nd East Lancashire Division, it became the first of the Territorial Divisions to deploy for overseas service. With the Division went the three Field Ambulances. These were not the first Manchester Medics to deploy for overseas service. That honour went to Number 18 Special Reserve Field Ambulance[14] which, on 10 September 1914 (as 42nd Division embarked from Southampton) disembarked in France with the 6th Division.

Kitchener wanted to use the TF to release regular troops garrisoned abroad for service on the fighting fronts. Thus the 42nd Division went to Egypt with the 43rd, 44th and 45th TF Divisions being sent to India, however it would not be long before TF Divisions would find their way to France [5, 20].

The stories of the Manchester Medics during the Great War would more than fill the pages of this book. From 2nd Western General Hospital which grew to be the largest home based Military Hospital of the War [14], to the Field Ambulances that provided medical support in Egypt, Gallipoli, Sinai, Mesopotamia, France and Flanders.

When the Great War is mentioned, the pictures that often spring to mind are of the cold damp trenches, the shell cratered no-man's

---

14 Although a Special Reserve Unit No 18 Field Ambulance was staffed by Officers and Men of the East Lancashire TF who had volunteered for Imperial Service overseas.

land and men lining up waiting to go 'over the top', many never to return. Many myths and legends have grown out of that time, none more so than that of the Somme. Often used as an example of the incompetence and ruthlessness of the Generals, with thousands of casualties sustained for no apparent gain. However, without the Battle of the Somme, Germany would have been able to reinforce their attack on the French at Verdun[15], probably breaking though the French lines and that may well have resulted in Germany winning the war. What cannot be argued are the casualty figures; at the end of that first sunny day in July over 19,000 British men lay dead in the fields of France. With such vast numbers it is difficult sometimes to image each one as an individual, as a father, husband, brother or son. Here, therefore, are some of the stories of the individuals who served with the Manchester Medics.

42nd Division's mission in Egypt was twofold; to relieve garrison troops for duty in Europe and to complete their training. Kitchener then intended for the Division to join the BEF in Europe. However, events in 1915 would find the Division moving further east rather

Figure 8 Colonel John Bently Mann and other Staff Officers at the installation of Husain Kamil as the Sultan of Egypt, Sovereign of Nubia, of the Sudan, of Kordofan and Darfur on 20 December 1914

---

15   Verdun was of great sentimental importance to the French. If it had fallen France may very well have fallen too. Verdun was the longest battle of the Great War and casualties figures for all sides numbered 800,000.

than west. In late April orders were received to join the Mediterranean Expeditionary Force in the Dardanelles under the command of General Sir Ian Hamilton. The Dardanelles campaign or Gallipoli as it is better known was aimed at putting Turkey out of the war. In reality, it became one of the biggest British military disasters of the war. [19]

Travelling with the East Lancashire Field Ambulances (ELFA) as their ADMS was Lieutenant Colonel John Bently Mann. He was aged fifty-two and had served with the TF for over twenty five years during which time he commanded 1st ELFA and Number 18 Special Reserve Field Ambulance. He was a successful surgeon with rooms on St John's Street in Manchester. His first wife, Hannah had died but he had remarried. So when he embarked with 42nd Division in September 1914 he left behind his wife Amelia, his young son Jack and his daughter, Mabel from his first marriage. [6, 21]

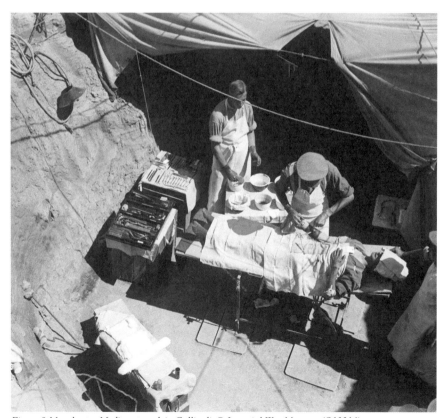

Figure 9 Manchester Medics at work in Gallipoli. © Imperial War Museum (Q13316)

Gallipoli was very different to the fields of France and Belgium. The peninsular was mountainous and the high ground was controlled by the Turks. Even the rest areas could not escape bombardment or the threat of snipers. All supplies, including water, had to be shipped in. As the campaign progressed into the summer and the temperature rose, disease became the biggest enemy. During the ten months of the campaign nearly 30,000 admissions to hospital were recorded for dysentery. This was well over twice as many as the next highest admission group, that of diarrhoea, which was just over 10,000. Of the casualties who contracted dysentery, the majority returned to duty, 811 died and 124 were evacuated. In late June of 1915 Lieutenant Colonel Mann contracted dysentery and became one of the 124 evacuated. As he made his way home, more Manchester Medics were readying themselves for the journey out to Gallipoli as part of the draft to reinforce 42nd Division. [22, 23]

Figure 10 Lieutenant Colonel H C Parker commanding 1st/1st East Lancashire Field Ambulance dressing the wounds of a Turkish soldier. © Imperial War Museum (Q13258)

In September of 1914 the War Office gave permission for the TF to form Second and later Third Line units and so the Manchester Medics recruited three Second Line Field Ambulances and three Third Line Field Ambulances. These Second and Third Lines would provide drafts for the First Line until 1917, when the Second Line Field Ambulances departed for France with the 66th East Lancashire Division. [5, 6, 20]

2nd/2nd ELFA would be raised from Burnley men under the command of Captain Callam. This unit became known locally as 'Callam's Own' and in November 1914, answering a newspaper call for volunteers, three young Burnley lads presented themselves for enlistment: Arthur Gilbert Altham aged 16, Regimental Number 516, Harry Ingham Hodskinson aged 17, Regimental Number 528, and Tom Alcock aged 15, Regimental Number 538. Of the three only Harry was legally old enough to join the TF. Arthur and Tom both worked in the cotton industry and Harry was a photographer by profession. [24]

On mobilisation in 1914, the men of the Field Ambulances had first been billeted at the Kings Road depot before being transferred to a camp near Hollingworth Lake, Littleborough. When the bulk of the Field Ambulances embarked for Egypt in September, the remaining troops formed the nucleus of the Second Line. It was probably here that the three young Burnley lads found themselves in late November of 1914 along with a newly commissioned Medical Officer (MO) Lieutenant Charles Bertram Marshall who had been posted in to 2nd/3rd ELFA. [17]

Training consisted mainly of route marches and stretcher drills, and when the units moved to Southport they were given the charge of a small hospital. Their medical training was given in the form of lectures from the unit MOs. [17]

These qualified men placed before us a banquet of food for the mind, and if we sometimes suffered from mental indigestion, we did do our best to digest the very many tasty morsels laid before us. [17] page 10

Sergeant A E F Francis 2/3rd ELFA

In the summer of 1915 the Field Ambulances were moved to Crowborough, Sussex where the Second Line East Lancashire Division was being concentrated. From late May onwards requests were made for reinforcements for the First Line and from early June men began to depart for the East. In late July our three Burnley lads including 67 other members of 2nd/2nd ELFA departed England for overseas service with 42nd Division in Gallipoli. Arthur, Harry and Tom were still below the legal minimum age for overseas service. The newly appointed Commanding Officer (CO) of 2nd/3rd ELFA, Captain CB Marshall along with 52 of his officers and men also departed for

43

service with the first line. In total 170 officers and men of the ELFA[s] embarked on the troop ship Royal Edward in late July 1915 en route for Gallipoli. [17, 24]

After a short stop over at Alexandria, Egypt, the Royal Edward departed on 12 August for Mudros, the main staging post for troops bound for Gallipoli. The danger of attack by submarine was an ever present threat and on the morning of 13 August the crew and troops practiced life boat drills. Shortly after the drill was completed, with most of the crew and soldiers below deck stowing equipment, the ship was struck astern by a torpedo and sank in just six minutes. Along with its crew and men of the ELFA[s] (destined for 42nd Division) the Royal Edward was also carrying a draft for the 29th Division numbering nearly 1,000 men. 54th (East Anglian) Casualty Clearing Station, men of the East Anglian, Highland and West Lancashire Field Ambulances (approximately 400[16] from medical units) and two interpreters of the 53rd Division. [24, 25]

Captain Charles Bertram Marshall was last seen with the Captain on the bridge of the Royal Edward as described by Lieutenant F B Smith of 2nd/3rd ELFA who was also on-board:

Of the 50 men of our Ambulance, only 3 are lost. I have not told you what a corporal of our section has told me, that he saw Captain Marshall, long after he himself was in the water, still on the highest deck with the captain of the ship, revolver in hand, encouraging and controlling the men. He had no need to use his weapon because discipline was splendid. The men knew his worth and not one but has spoken to me sadly of our loss. Such a cool courageous "sticking to duty" was characteristic of the man he was. [26]

The news of the loss of the Royal Edward was met with great sorrow back home:

In the midst of our stay in Peas Pottage much gloom settled over the camp on receipt of the news that the Field Ambulance was called upon to mourn its first casualties, several of our comrades who had gone out on draft to the First Line having been drowned in the sinking of the ill-fated transport ship "Royal Edward," en route for

---

16 It should not be assumed that all these men were members of the RAMC some would have been members of the Army Service Corps.

Egypt. We had lost our former Commanding Officer, Captain CB Marshall, and Privates Black, Davies, Fisher and Simms.

Captain Marshall had been a really good CO, a much respected gentleman, a man who would have ornamented any profession, an officer of outstanding worth, and his passing was accepted by every member of the Field Ambulance as a personal and tragic loss.

He was;

"One who never turned his back, but marched breast forward."

During his connection with the Unit, he had shown a deep interest in the welfare of the men under his command and in every action it was easy to observe that he was sincere, upright, fearless, and wholly absorbed in his duty. [17] page 14

Sergeant A E F Francis 2/3ʳᵈ ELFA

Charles Marshall was just 26 years old. Fifty eight other men of the East Lancashire Field Ambulances are believed to have perished on the Royal Edward including Arthur Altham and Tom Alcock.

The Burnley Express carried the following piece on 14 September 1915

Private Arthur Gilbert Altham's parents received official intimation at 28 Cromwell Street on Thursday morning. Private Altham was only seventeen years of age, and joined what is known as "Callam's Own" in October. He was an old St Peter's Day and Sunday school pupil and after leaving day school he continued his studies at the evening classes, gaining exhibitions which kept him there. He was particularly studying cotton work and at the same time as he enlisted was learning the jacquard trade at Grey's Mill. He was the youngest child of the family and his feared loss has occasioned his parents much distress ......

The following letter has been received from his former Sunday School Teacher:-

The County Bank House, Haslingden, September 1st 1915. Dear Mrs Altham, - only last evening I heard that Arthur was thought to be on the Royal Edward, and I write to express my sympathy with you in all your anxiety and trouble. When the other day I sent to you Arthur's "Bible reading Union Notes" I little thought that he was amongst the victims of that sad disaster. Indeed, I did not know that he had left England. There is still a possibility that he is amongst the rescued, and for your sake I hope it may be so; but if, in God's providence, has been taken away, I do not think that anyone I have known would be more ready for the call than Arthur. He was a thoughtful and good lad, and I am sure you will feel the anxiety and strain of suspense very much. – with sympathy, yours faithfully, Harold Holden". [24]

Only 500 of the 1,500 on board survived including Harry Hodskinson. He joined his new unit 1st/2nd ELFA in Gallipoli remaining there until January 1916 when the campaign was abandoned and 42nd Division returned to Egypt.

Figure 11 *Private Arthur Gilbert Altham*   Figure 12 *Private Tom Alcock*

When he returned home to Manchester in the summer of 1915, Lieutenant Colonel Mann found an extensive system of military medical care that today would be difficult to imagine. By November 1914, 2nd Western General Hospital already had 843 beds located at its Headquarters, the newly build Central School on Whitworth Street having 445 beds, the others being located at the Day Training College on Princess Street and the School of Domestic Economy[17]

---

17 The School of Domestic Economy is now part of the Manchester Metropolitan University

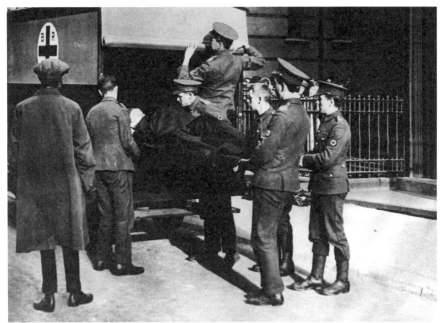

Figure 13 Unloading casualties at 2nd Western General Hospital Headquarters on Whitworth Street

on High Street. There were another 1146 beds available for use by the military in civilian hospitals in and around the Manchester area, including Blackburn to the north and Winsford to the south. A further 1,100 beds were provided by the Red Cross Hospitals. 2nd Western received its first patients on 16 August 1914 and its first casualties from the front on 20 September, by the end of November it had admitted 5,560 casualties including German prisoners and officers and men of the Belgian Army. [14, 27]

The nursing staff, which is under the charge of Miss Fletcher, aided by the 'principal matron' Miss Sparshott, has been gradually raised to 141. Many of the 'sisters' are highly qualified and have held important positions; not a few have been matrons of small hospitals; several have seen military surgery during the Balkans War. It has, however, not been easy to obtain the required numbers, and undoubtedly the hospitals are understaffed in this respect. A very heavy responsibility has fallen upon many of the sisters, as there has been no resident staff, while it was quite impossible for the 'a la suite' officers to perform the majority of dressings or to carry on the usual duties of the house surgeons.[27]

At the outbreak of the war there were only 297 Regular nurses of the Queen Alexandra's Imperial Military Nursing Service (QAIMNS) augmented by members of the QAIMNS reservists and Territorial Force Nursing Service (TFNS). Although the number of Regular QAIMNS did not increase[18] by the end of the war 11,000 reservists and 8,140 TFNS had volunteered. Of the TFNS 2,280 serviced overseas. Prior to the war, the War Office had started a scheme of voluntary aid organisations called Voluntary Aid Detachments (VAD). They were raised by the County Territorial Association and organised by the British Red Cross Society. The majority of the work of the VAD was in the provision and running of hospitals and convalescent homes for war casualties. These were mainly located in large houses that people had donated the use of for the duration of the war. There were however, more unusual hospital buildings; the Royal Lancashire Agricultural Society put their pavilion that they used for their annual show at the disposal of the VAD The pavilion was moved from Blackburn to a site on Moor Park, Preston where it was erected and adapted for the treatment of 35 patients. By the end of the war and after several donations from private and business sources the hospital at Moor Park could accommodate 270 patients. [28, 29]

"..... The nurse is the one who is allowed to see patients at their weakest moments, to tend friends in their darkest hours, to bring unseen strength by giving of her own strength...." [16] page 89

Miss M E Sparshott CBE RRC

As well as nurses and VAD travelling from East Lancashire for service overseas, many travelled to Lancashire to work in the Military and VAD hospitals. People like Gertrude and Nora Giltinan who travelled from Cork, Ireland to work as VADs in Manchester. Lydia Grant had also crossed water to reach Manchester but her journey had been slightly longer, since Lydia was from Brisbane, Australia. There were many females working with the Australian Medical Services. After working in hospitals and on-board hospital ships in support of the Gallipoli Campaign and later in Egypt they moved to Europe when the Australian and New Zealand Army Corps (ANZAC) transferred to the Western Front in 1916 [29]. Why Lydia ended up in Manchester is

---

18 This was a deliberate act to prevent the problem of what to do with a large surplus of nursing staff at the end of the war.

unclear but two of her brothers were serving with the Australian Army in France.

Although there were male members of the VAD the majority were female who would turn their hand to any task required of them. There were very few qualified nurses in the VAD although they were all given training in First Aid and nursing, their jobs would include anything from cooking and cleaning, to driving ambulances, to assisting with clerical work [29]. In late March of 1916 Lydia found herself as a patient admitted to 2nd Western General Hospital, Ducie Avenue School on Denmark Street[19]. On 28 March it was reported that she was being treated in the hospital for measles that had turned to Septic Arthritis and although her condition was improving her brothers had been sent for. On 30 March she lapsed in to unconsciousness and on 1 April, with her brother Chesborough at her side she died. Her name does not appear in the records of the Commonwealth War Graves Commission[20] but she is remembered by the Manchester Medics. Her name along with five other VADs and two nurses appears on the Great War Memorial in the Drill Hall on Kings Road. You will find her name just below that of Gertrude Giltinan who died in the same hospital of Influenza on 19 November 1918[21].

In late December 1916 came the news that the 2nd Line Field Ambulances were to deploy with the 66th Division to France. For the last twelve months of their training $2^{nd}/3^{rd}$ ELFA had the advantage of being commanded by Lieutenant Colonel Holt who had seen active service in Gallipoli, and who, due to injury, could no longer deploy on active service. [17, 20]

Figure 14 Lieutenant Colonel Thomas Holt

---

19 Many schools in Manchester were taken over by 2nd Western General Hospital during the war and converted for hospital use. The use of educational facilities was met with some degree of criticism at the time. Ducie Avenue School had 240 beds.
20 The Commonwealth War Graves Commission commemorates those who have died in service or the causes of death can be attributed to service during World Wars One and Two.
21 Of the seven female names on the Great War Memorial, four died between 8 October 1918 and 3 January 1919 of Influenza

……..when he was not allowed to accompany us to France because of disability left by wounds on his previous foreign service, and we left him behind a lonely figure on a railway platform, there were some who said, and we think with accuracy, tears were streaming down the face of the tall war-injured officer. [17] page 25

Sergeant A E F Francis 2/3rd ELFA describing Lieutenant Colonel Holt

Many injured men like Holt would find themselves employed in useful, if at times frustrating, war roles back home. Holt's combat experience would be of more value to the men of 2nd/3rd ELFA than anything they would read in a book or be taught by instructors who had never seen active service. Lieutenant Colonel Mann also found himself employed in support of the war effort as a Medical Board officer for the selection of new recruits. He would perform this roll until he was forced to retire due to ill health. He relinquished his commission on 22 August 1917 and died on 15 January 1918 from a cerebral haemorrhage and exhaustion brought on by the infection he had contracted in Gallipoli [23]. The grief of the Mann family was made worse by the fact that his second wife Amelia had died the previous year leaving behind Mable to look after her young brother Jack.

2nd/3rd ELFA were granted final leave between 11 and 22 February and they embarked on 1st March 1917 bound for Le Havre, France. At the same time 42nd Division were arriving at Marseilles, France. [17, 19]

42nd Division had left behind the sun and heat of the desert for one of the worst winters Europe had ever experienced, described in the railway journey from Marseilles to Pont Remy:

Men, who had at much cost become acclimatised to the intense heat and dryness of the Sinai Desert, were suddenly plunged into the opposite extreme of an arctic climate……..

…….. The troops detrained at Pont Remy in a storm of snow and sleet, and marched through deep, freezing slush to the villages in which billets had been prepared. [19] page 86

One of the roles of the RAMC was to provide bathing and washing facilities for the troops. This was a mammoth task as described in Number 18 Special Reserve Field Ambulance's War Diary of December 1914:

The capacity is for between 5000 and 6000 hot baths per week and also the washing of towels, shirts, socks and under wear. [30]

One of the first tasks of 2nd/3rd ELFA was to take over the running of the Divisional baths, which could cater for three or four hundred men at once. The CO had insisted that all men should have clean shirts and pants; came the day the stores were near empty, the Quarter Master's Department engaged in the 'creative resourcefulness ' that they are still well known for even today:

Gregory sent out his scouts. Prowling about at the Rail Head they found a big truck load of new garments which had been consigned to another Division. Without delay, the scouts returned and related to Gregory the good news. Of course, it did not take long to transfer the information to Lieutenant Bounds, nor did it take Lieutenant Bounds long to get hold of the stuff and stow it away in the stock rooms of the Baths. Thus we early scrounged to good purpose, and the Quartermaster gave evidence that his audacity was now approaching ripeness. [17] page 52

Sergeant A E F Francis 2/3rd ELFA

Later in the war, during the great retreat of 1918, Captain Bound would volunteer to take transport up to an Advanced Dressing Station (ADS) that was in danger of being overrun by the enemy. Travelling under heavy bombardment he and his men not only rescued 22 officers and men who thought escape was impossible, but also the medical stores and equipment of the ADS which allowed it to re-open elsewhere. He was awarded the Military Cross for his "courage and resource". [17]

In late August of 1917, 42nd Division made its way to the village of Watou, a short distance from Ypres. Before the war this ancient city was famous for its Cloth Hall and fine linen exports. By 1917, it had almost been raised to the ground and invoked different thoughts in the minds of the British soldier and civilian population alike:

Ypres stood for death and mutilation and agony, and all that was most cruel and horrible in war. To wives and parents it was the Valley of the Shadow of Death, where their husbands and sons fought a never-ending fight with the Powers of Darkness, and never gave ground, yet never gained the victory. [19] page 97

The Third Battle of Ypres (also known as the Battle of Passchendaele) had begun in fine weather in late July, with heavy bombardment of the German lines, but by the time it came for troops to attack heavy rain had turned the area into an enormous quagmire. On 1 September, 42nd Division passed through the Menin Gate bound for the Ypres salient. Frederick Gibbon describes what they encountered:

> *No part of it was ever at rest. By day, aircraft sought to spot every movement that was attempted on either side, and day and night the guns sprayed the trenches, the roads, the duckboard paths, with shrapnel and high explosives, the grim resolve to kill dominating every other thought or desire. The ghastly evidences of the fighting in three great battles and nearly three years of warfare were brought to light by the bombardments that tore and flung up the earth. [19] page 99*

The war diary of $1^{st}/2^{nd}$ ELFA, whose Headquarters (HQ) was located at Red Farm, Brandhoek, west of Ypres, describes the wounded that began to arrive:

> **1 Sept 1917 9pm** *Nothing special to note: wounded have been coming in a continuous stream the past 24 hours: wounded nearly all shell wounds*

> **5 Sept 1917 9pm** *Gassed cases in numbers today: mustard gas: symptoms chiefly are nausea conjunctivitis of the eyes erythema and blistering of skin especially on parts where the skin perspires more than in other ...... Secret orders for a stunt tomorrow morning and preparations accordingly made. [31]*

On 6 September, 125th Brigade of the 42nd Division attacked Iberian, Borry and Beck House Farm. The attack failed with the loss of nearly 800 officers and men. Gibbon describes the conditions and some of the actions of members of the Field Ambulance:

> *Sergeant J H Ashton, 3rd Field Ambulance, worked unceasingly and without rest for forty-eight hours, often under heavy fire, in charge of squads removing the wounded.*

> *..... the Advanced Dressing Stations at Railway Dugout, Bavaria House and Potijze Chateau were cramped for space and were frequently gassed and always shelled......[19] pages 101and 104*

At some time between 9 and 10 of September, Harry Hodskinson was wounded by shell fire. He died of his wounds on 10 September and was buried at Brandhoek. He had survived the sinking of the Royal Edward[22], had lived through the harsh winter of the Dardanelles. He had seen the Pyramids of Egypt and served in the heat of the Sinai and yet was only 20 years old.

On 22 September 1917 the Burnley Express published the following:

Dr Purves of Burnley who is serving with the R.A.M.C. wrote on the 15th inst.:- "I have intended writing for some days but have had no opportunity and now seize the first chance to express my very sincere regret and also voice the deep feelings of sorrow of the officers and other ranks of this Field Ambulance. I was with your boy at the time and really cannot get over his death. It was a fatal wound, no suffering. He was unconscious from the beginning. A small piece from a shell bursting a little way from our dressing station fell through a small opening in a cellar dugout where we were stationed and hit your boy in the head. I had him brought back and buried in a military cemetery. We are placing a cross over the grave and a wreath of coloured beads." [24]

Figure 15 Private Harry Ingham Hodskinson

Several other letters were written to Harry's family, and all were at pains to point out that he had been buried and his grave marked. Today this may seem odd but when read in the context of nearly one million having no known grave; the relevance of this fact becomes apparent.

Histories of any war tend to be sombre affairs, and rightly so, but for those who have experienced war, it is not always the intense life and death situation that people imagine. Sometimes it is boring, sometimes it brings great joy – a letter, a parcel or just the company of friends. In 1931 Sergeant Alfred E F Francis wrote a book, "The History of

---

22 Of the 34 Burnley survivors of the Royal Edward three others as well as Harry would not live to see the end of the war

the 2nd/3rd East Lancashire Field Ambulance". It opens a window onto a group of Manchester Medics who journeyed though 'Hell Fire Corner' and back, and despite it all not only retained their spirit but that singular peculiar characteristic of the British Medic – their quirky sense of humour. It is only fitting to leave the last words of this chapter to him.

In March 1918 the Germans launched a major offensive across the whole of the Western Front. As the British Army rapidly retreated, valuable equipment had to be removed from a particularly dangerous point in 2nd/3rd ELFA lines where the following conversation took place:

"Now then, Flitcroft[23], do you want to gain distinction?" cried S/Sgt-Major Farndale.

"I don't mind distinction, Sergeant-Major," was the retort, *"but I don't want extinction!"*

Figure 16 1st/2nd Field Ambulance taken some time in 1916. The picture includes Harry Hodskinson and other survivors of the Royal Edward

---

23 Flitcroft gained neither distinction or extinction but after the war emigrated to Canada

The TA between the Wars (1919-1939)

"I have no doubt that cuts must fall heavily on the Territorial Army, but I am alarmed at the rumours floating about, which include a drastic reduction in the length of annual training, and even go as far as the actual abolition of the Force"[5]page93

Earl of Scarbrough (Chairman of the East Riding Territorial Association and former Director General of the Territorial Army)

The Territorial Force in the Great War had fought on every front and won many battle honours, both individual, battalion and divisional but the end of the War would bring its biggest battle: a fight for its very survival.

The TF was disbanded at the end of the War, with a promise from the Secretary of State for War, Sir Winston Churchill, that it would be reconstituted. This would be difficult since the priorities facing Britain in 1919 were very different from those she faced in the pre-war years. No one could envisage a large scale war happening at any time soon, and the threat of invasion from Germany had disappeared. The focus for the Army was the defence of the Empire and to counter the threat from the new Bolshevik Government in Russia. Its pre-war terms of service meant that the TF could not be compulsorily mobilised for overseas service, and since the threat of invasion had gone, there was no longer a need for a Home Defence force. Why keep the TF if it had no immediate use, when there were so many other demands on the country's finances, such as social and welfare reforms and investing in the country's infrastructure after the war? For the TF to be reformed it would need to accept new terms of service.

Although the TF could now be mobilised for overseas service in a National Emergency, other changes in the terms of service were advantageous. There had been talk before the Great War of changes to pay and the introduction of a yearly payment (a bounty) if certain training objectives were met. This did not meet with universal approval since it would damage the 'volunteer spirit' and might attract the 'wrong sort of men' who would join for personal gain as opposed to a sense of civic duty. In 1920 the argument for changes to pay was won and not only would there be an annual bounty of up to £5.00 but during annual training Camp they would receive pay at Regular Army rates[24]. [5] In 1921 the Territorial Force was renamed the Territorial Army and the old Special Reserve became the Militia. The Militia was needed to provide the Regular Army with reinforcements when conditions were such that the TA could not, in law, be mobilised. The TA had become a Second Line that could only be mobilised for overseas service under strict conditions, and would only be deployed as whole units. [5]

But what of Home Defence? The threat of external invasion had gone but what about the threat from within? The early 1920s saw great upheaval in British society, and mass unemployment brought about civil unrest. With this in mind, Churchill attempted to include in the new TA Terms of Service a clause that allowed them to be used to assist civil powers. He failed, but he later tried to use existing Terms of Service to mobilise the TA for use in civil disputes. He again failed, however members of the TA were asked to volunteer for service in aid of the civil powers on two occasions between 1921 and 1926. The first was during the Miners' Strike of April 1921, when men left their Territorial units and joined the Defence Force which was being raised to support the police, and again during the General Strike of 1926, with the formation of the Civil Constabulary Reserve. These two forces (The Defence Force and The Civil Constabulary Reserve) played little part in the disputes they were raised to combat since by the time they were fully operational both strikes had collapsed. [5, 32]

With the reconstitution of the TA, Manchester saw the return of the three Field Ambulances, the General Hospital and the emergence of a Casualty Clearing Station (CCS) [6]. However it would not be long before pressure to reduce military spending would reach the Manchester Medics.

The Great War had brought with it a new kind of warfare that had created a fear among the British civilian population that would last long after the war was over. In December 1914, the British mainland experienced German bombing raids for the first time. This was to greatly influence defence spending in the run-up to the Second World War (WW2) [33].

---

24 This was not as good as it seems, the Regular Army rate of pay was less than the average civilian wage.

For many years after 1919 the prospect of another major war was thought impossible and the annual defence spending reflected this view. Furthermore in the unlikely event of the country being attacked the threat would not come by sea but by air [33]. Thus, whilst the new Royal Air Force (RAF) experienced a high degree of investment and growth, the Army reduced in size, resulting in the disbandment of many units. The Regular Army suffered more than the TA from the reduction in defence spending but even so the cut backs for the TA were difficult and sometimes painful to bear.

In order to maintain a volunteer presence throughout the country, all 14 TA Divisions would remain, but with reduced numbers. Within 42nd Division, this was met with 'dismay and anger' for, whilst other Divisions failed to recruit, it was the strongest in the country. It was still asked to merge the 6th and 7th Manchester Battalions [5]. With no major war expected within ten years there was a reduced need for Service Support Corps such as the Signals, Army Service Corps and Army Medical Services. By 1935, the East Lancashire Territorial Medical Services consisted of a Divisional Headquarters with one Regular RAMC officer and three other ranks. The three Field Ambulances had been re-named to follow suit with the Division's infantry Brigades. 125th Field Ambulance (the amalgamation of the three Field Ambulances) had six officers, 103 other ranks and no permanent staff, and 12th (2nd Western) General Hospital had ten Officers, 100 other ranks and no permanent staff [6]. Although rearmament had begun in 1935 due to the growing threat posed by Germany, the TA continued to suffer from lack of funds and equipment, with the exception of the two Divisions that had converted to Anti-Aircraft duties. These two Divisions were experiencing the building of new Drill Halls, increased recruitment and equipment levels [33, 34]. It was not until the eve of WW2 that the Government decided to increase the strength of both the Regular Army and the TA and it would not be long before they would once again embark for mainland Europe in defence of France and Flanders.

Figure 17 1937 winners of the TA Ambulance Challenge Shield held at Millbank London. From left to right Corporal N Ryder, Private G Bradder, Private C Timms and Private H A Cockcroft

Of the four men above Corporal Ryder deployed as a Sergeant with 125 Field Ambulance in April 1940 and joined the BEF in Europe; Private Hector Armitage Cockcroft died 29 October 1944 whilst serving as a Staff Sergeant with 8 Field Dressing Station. He is buried in Jonkbos war cemetery, Nijmegen in the Netherlands.

World War Two (1939-1945)

In February 1939 I was told a Major Toothill was to form two units of RAMC for Anti – Aircraft Command. RSM Fagg of the Regulars arrived, and as the Drill Hall was full, we were moved to Urmston Grammar School where all our initial training was carried out. We soon were being taught the intricacies of the Thomas Splint.

Came the day for our kit to be issued; first the kit bag to stuff everything into as you moved down the line. Service Dress with knee-length puttees needing to be carefully applied to avoid restricting the circulation. Cap badge, brass, RAMC, numerals and a letter "T" for Territorial. A sad day after the war began when we lost the T. We were proud to be Terries.

July 1939, the first camp for a month's intensive training. Half the unit moved to the East Coast to a Searchlight Unit for the Royal Artillery. The other half of the unit arrived on 15 August little knowing they would not be released until 1946.

Major (Ret'd) John Mee

In 1938, many TA units converted temporarily to a searchlight role. By 1940, all such units transferred to the Royal Artillery. The Government decided in early 1939, to double the size of the TA, and on 31 March 1939 the War Office authorised the "duplication" of all units. The TA mobilised on 1 September 1939, its units embodied, and lost all independent distinction from the Regular Army for the duration of the war. When the Army demobilised in 1946, its former TA units were temporarily suspended, re-forming in 1947.

Lessons had been learnt from the mobilisation process employed prior and during the Great War. Significant in this was that the TA, who had acquitted themselves very well during the Great War, would become a major focus of any new mobilisation. There would be no New Armies, all volunteers and conscripts would be assimilated into Regular and TA units. For new volunteers the Kings Road depot was the first stop in their army service.

Interviewer: You weren't obviously medically trained

Tom: No not at all

Interviewer: So when you enlisted or you signed up that day, this was prior to the Second World War?

Tom: It was in early May 1939, because I would have been called up for National Service, so I thought I would pre-empt that

Interviewer: You saw the writing on the wall?

Tom: The writing was on the wall

Interviewer: Was there a steady trickle of gentlemen – guys joining up at that time?

Tom: An avalanche

Interviewer: An avalanche?

Tom: An avalanche – in all those recruiting centres – an avalanche

Interviewer: For the same reasons: they saw it coming?

Tom: Unemployment after the recession was going down but there was still a lot of unemployed about – people weren't trained for anything and I suppose they thought they might as well join the army anyway

Interviewer: So did you sign up as a Territorial?

Tom: Yes

Interviewer: Who did you sign up with; obviously 207 wasn't there?

Tom: 127 Field Ambulance

Interviewer: Was that the only unit there at the time?

Tom: No there was 125, 126, 127 the 5th Western General, the 7th Western General[25] hospitals and 12 CCS.

Interviewer: So how did you end up with that particular Field Ambulance?

Tom: I went into that queue

Interviewer: As simple as that!

Major Tom Howell

---

25 Tom's recollections may not be precise as 7th Western General Hospital did not come in to existence until 1947. The hospital being referred to here is more likely to be 12th (2nd Western) General Hospital.

The Territorial Army Medical Services had been reformed following the Great War on similar lines, in that the medical services based at Kings Road were in support of 42nd Infantry Division which was to form part of the BEF sent to France at the outbreak of World War Two (WW2). 125, 126 and 127 Field Ambulances and 12 CCS accompanied the Division and remained in France during the "Phoney War". The 2nd (Western) General Hospital of the Great War had been replaced by 12th (2nd Western) General Hospital which mobilised to Ormskirk and eventually went to Egypt to become 61st General Hospital [35].

Tom Howell was one of the first volunteers in this wave of enthusiasm to "get the job done". Like the generation before him, the desire to serve overcame any anxieties; that were to follow:

Tom: *From when I joined up in the May, in the June of course we had the fortnight's camp, which we went up to a place called Four Lane Ends – near Lancaster – between Lancaster and Morecambe. Where we had a fortnight camp there, that meant acclimatisation – boots, which a lot of people hated of course because they got blisters and everything. I was very fit when I joined up because for several years I had indulged in bike racing, time trials and things like that, - so that involved 25, 30 and 50 miles from time to time. You pushed off somewhere in Cheshire about 5 or 6 o'clock in the morning in summer – where you did your 25 miles. I used to do that an hour and fifteen minutes – So I was very fit when I joined.*

Interviewer: *So that took you through the summer and obviously war was declared in September.*

Tom: *They took us to Annual Camp then. That is worth describing to you – that's where they hammered us, 16 to a bell tent woe betide a man who slept where the door was, you know. It was lots of fun and games lots of banter going on, the food was foul.*

Interviewer: *How many in the Field Ambulance?*

Tom: *234 was the War Establishment.*

Interviewer: *And when you joined, there or there abouts?*

Tom: *It filled up very, very quickly, filled up very quickly.*

Interviewer: *So you were exercising on camp for full deployment – all key people?*

Figure 18 Bomb damage to the Jewish Hospital (Courtesy of Manchester Libraries, Information and Archives, Manchester City Council)

Figure 20 German casualties from Norway being unloaded at 5th (Western) General Hospital (Courtesy of Trafford General Hospital)

Figure 19 Bomb damage to Sparshott House, the nurses' recreation hall at Manchester Royal Infirmary, October 1940

Figure 21 The RSM and members of the nursing staff of 5th (Western) General Hospital (Courtesy of Trafford General Hospital)

Tom: *That's right; the CO then was a man with the initials W A R – W A Ramsey*
Interviewer: *Very appropriate*
Major Tom Howell

The War quickly came to the people of Manchester in the form of the Blitz. The many civilian casualties put increasing pressure on the local health and emergency services.

To some extent, civilians replaced soldiers as casualties and the hospitals were not exempt from bombing; many of them including Manchester Royal Infirmary[26] and Hope Hospital suffering considerable damage

---

26 Miss Sparshott had been influential in raising money for the building of the hall pictured above, a large part of the funding being provided by the nurses themselves. Sparshott died on 9 October 1940 two days before the hall was bombed. It was rebuilt after the war and bore the name Sparshott. It was demolished in the early years of the 21st Century during redevelopment of the MRI and surrounding hospitals.

and with many nurses and doctors killed or injured [36][27]. As in the Great War, many of the local hospitals gave over beds to the military. At the outbreak of WW2 Park Hospital, Davyhulme[28] became a military hospital with the title, 5th (Western) General Hospital. Many of the staff came from the ranks of the Manchester Medics and it was commanded by Colonel Daniel Dougal, MC, TD, a Professor working at St Mary's Hospital and TA officer. In 1943 the command of the hospital passed in to American hands and it became No. 10 Station Hospital.

Michael Coates tells of 207's founder, his Grandfather Sir William Coates' war time experience, not unfamiliar to many families at that time:

...and we moved beds down to the cellar and slept there. Providentially nothing hit the house. Incendiary bombs landed all around but if they had hit the house there was no one to look after it. But the house was not hit, and there we were, but it was quite a strange existence. And obviously, although I didn't realise it, they were very worried about the whole situation, very worried about my father who was out in the Far East, and Jackie's father; he was killed. But she was very young then; she hardly remembers him, if she remembers him at all. So it was a very anxious time for them and I was not particularly aware how anxious they must have been.

Colonel Sir William Coates, then aged 79, came to see the Manchester units off to war, and was there to see them back at the end.

The medical services in WW2, as in the Great War, comprised of large numbers of Territorial Army volunteers. In the inter-war years, new weapon systems, particularly high explosive shells delivered by artillery and air, were developed. Advances in medicine and surgery had ensured that the Army Medical Services had significantly modernised its doctrine especially in regard to the treatment of "secondary shock" and how this could considerably improve mortality

---

27 In the week leading up to Christmas 1940 bombing took the lives of 14 nurses at the Salford Royal, six lives at Hope Hospital including the medical superintendent, matron and the head porter and the Jewish Hospital lost five members of staff.
28 This Hospital later became the first National Health Service Hospital and is now known as Trafford General Hospital.

rates[29]. Transfusions of blood and intravenous fluids were encouraged and an increased appreciation of evacuation time lines to surgery, were to be established[30].

The 1935 RAMC Training Handbook outlined where lessons learnt in the Great War had still had to be revised for the Second:

In modern mobile warfare, one of the belligerents prepares and delivers an attack which, if successful, will generally mean an advance for a distance which varies according to the military situation, after which there is halt of at least some days duration, to prepare for the next attack. The medical services will thus in all probability have short intervals to clear all sick and wounded and get ready for the next action. [37] page 195

The BEF felt the full force of the German Blitzkrieg and were exposed to extreme difficulties due to the rapid German advance and having its chain of evacuation of casualties significantly hindered;

Tom: *.....then of course the war in France, the phoney war as it was – then we went over to France in April 40.*

Interviewer: *Was it 42 Div that went?*

Tom: *42 Div went yea. We went up – we were in training in France for a time at a place called Sailly Le Sec and from there we pushed onto the border, because things were brewing up there – so we were just short of the Belgian border, when as the saying was in those days 'the balloon went up' in other words the Blitzkrieg started......*

Interviewer: *Well you were there on the Belgian border and the balloon has gone up.*

Tom: *The balloon goes up and we are pushed forward and chaos reigned supreme we were routed literally.*

Major Tom Howell

Redmond McLaughlin's book, Famous Regiments edition 'The Royal Army Medical Corps' describes the chaos:

---

29 Primary and Secondary shock were a collection of symptoms relating to injury and encompassed a slight faint to severe haemorrhage. The above could be relieved by hot water bottles – to hot saline solutions given by the rectum.
30 Intravenous solutions were in their infancy and the hand book proclaimed that "the most valuable solution is gum saline"

But it was Dunkirk that troops of all arms were most severely tested, not least the RAMC. Evacuation was spasmodic. Ambulances arrived, but seldom was there a docked ship to receive their patients. There was little equipment but in a chateau basement a small operating theatre was kept going. Dressings, rations and even anaesthetics were in short supply.

On 1 June (1940) the men of 12 CCS believed that they were now the last medical unit still functioning around Dunkirk. Any idea of getting away had long since been banished. Then came the orders to leave three officers and thirty men to look after the 230 patients who could not be moved. Names were drawn from a hat..... "The three doctors took their fate splendidly and cheerfully, as did the men" [38] page 63

Major Philip Newman RAMC, a surgeon, was one of the lucky three doctors and his account can be read on BBC website, WW2 People's War (http://www.bbc.co.uk/ww2peopleswar/stories/15/a2310715.shtml).

Further along the beach Private Tom Howell is having a torrid time.

......he (James Hedridge)[31] and I were out hunting for food and we found a warehouse with a lot of bread that had gone mouldy, so we had two sacks with us and we were making our way back and when we got to the steel doors that led into the mall, we saw a "Froggy" pointing upwards, the Stukas were coming down more or less all the time, so we dropped our sacks and got in, closed the doors and there was a great crunch behind and when we got out about an hour later, we could see a great hole, we could have been in there. That's the luck of the draw, some soldiers make it some soldiers don't.....

.....the man in charge of the evacuation at that time was General Alexander and he came to see us, he was telling us what the situation was and how grave it was and then I piped up and said: " Do you think we will be captured sir" and he said: "Son they do not capture Generals so easily". So he outlined what we had to do: he said there would be two destroyers coming in, and do not forget this was the penultimate day of the evacuation, because the day after, it was officially finished. He said you would get lots of cases coming through, you must not take any stretcher cases,

---

31 James Hedridge survived the war and went onto be Town Clerk of Stockport

they will stay behind, he said because the Tyne Tees Division[32] had volunteered that their medical element will remain behind with them, they volunteered to do that, it was quite a sacrifice, because they were going to be in the bag for five or six years, something like that.

But he said (General Alexander):"as many of the walking wounded you can get on board, pack everywhere including the decks and you will get on this destroyer as well". So, well, all my colleagues of the unit had gone four days before, that was the Friday or the Saturday, they had to wade out, swim out to the things, we actually walked on board. It was a rough ride, the sister destroyer was thumped and went literally down in the harbour, and we made our way back to Dover harbour.

Interviewer: *Did the majority of the unit come back?*

Tom: *The majority, yea. I think we lost a cook. I cannot remember anyone else because the history of that is very vague.*

Major Tom Howell

Although the remnants of the units were collected back together, the personnel were assigned to other units and 125[33] and 126 were disbanded for the duration of the war. 127 were to form part of the new airborne brigade and in December 1942 became 127 Parachute Field Ambulance. The break-up was to allow experienced men to form the basis of new medical units to support initially Home Defence and then the offensive:

……I was called out and told "you are going to be posted now" …… " we been told now to post those elements who had seen service in France, and you will be posted to a unit called 163 Field Ambulance" They came from Norwich, they were nearly all shoe makers, and they were at Chester-Le-Street.

Private Tom Howell

---

32 Many RAMC facilities and their staff were left in Belgium and France to care for the wounded, including 17th General Hospital at Camiers. Many medical personnel became POWs instead of protected personnel under the Geneva Convention. (Longden, S, "Dunkirk: the men they left behind. 2009", London: Constable & Robinson Limited)

33 A large proportion of 125 Field Ambulance were captured en masse at Dunkirk

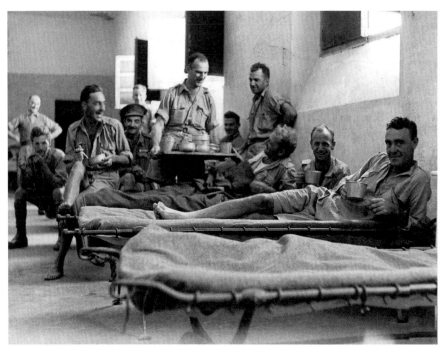

Figure 22 Staff Sergeant T Garratt serving lunch in Tobruk. As a Sergeant he was with 125 Field Ambulance when they joined the BEF in 1940. The story of his journey from Europe to Tobruk is not known

Lieutenant Colonel Otway gives a dramatic insight of the innovative medical concepts developed by the new airborne Field Ambulances such as 127 Parachute Field Ambulance:

Before the advent of airborne forces the Army had always worked upon the principle that a casualty should be picked up in battle by stretcher bearers, evacuated from the regimental aid post to a dressing station and then to progressively improving hospitals. Airborne forces accepted this principle as far as the Dressing Station but no further, in the initial stages of battle as it was impracticable. Normal evacuation was only possible after the ground forces had linked up with the airborne troops. But major surgical operations might have to be performed and therefore the only solution was to take the doctors and the surgical teams to the troops instead of vice versa. This is in fact what happened and the surgeons jumped with their instruments, often performing their operations in the front line. Airborne Field Ambulances held the casualties and kept them in good condition for eventual evacuation when conditions permitted. [39] pages 47-48

127 Parachute Field Ambulance subsequently accompanied the airborne brigade to North Africa and then to the invasion of Sicily and Italy. An Airborne Brigade, used gliders extensively; not everyone parachuted into combat. Subsequently, members of 127 were lost in July 1943, when the gliders they were in for the invasion of Sicily, ditched into the sea [2, 4]³⁴. More were later lost following the Italian invasion when the ship transporting them, HMS Abdeil, was torpedoed in Taranto Harbour in September 1943, with the loss of 129 men. The airborne brigade left Italy in 1943 to prepare for D-Day. 127 however were to remain in Italy and were used extensively throughout the campaign, some remaining in Italy until 1946 [39].

Tom Howell found himself in Italy (via North Africa) in 1943 with 104 General Hospital and then No.1 General Hospital, Rome.

Interviewer: *And what happened to 127 when you were out in Italy, do you know?*

Tom: *Well they were a glider borne Field Ambulance. In the attack to take Italy it was necessary to go to various other places first. First there was the island of Pantelleria and then the island of Sicily, before you could have a bash at the soft under belly there round about Solerno area, where it was suitable for infantry to land – and get the assault boats and things like that.*

Figure 23 Pencil drawing showing location of Pantelleria

Interviewer: *And this is where you were saying that a lot of them ditched.*

Tom: *Pantelleria, yes.*

Interviewer: *Where's Pantelleria?*

Tom: *You will have to look at the map of the Med.*

Interviewer: *It is a small island?*

Tom: *Ya, - there is Sicily there – you go this way going right*

---

34 Gliders landed in the sea with 252 reported drowned, RAMC numbers not included

along the coast and the island of Pantelleria is there. So they were over Pantelleria when they got a lot of flak from the Germans. The Americans were towing and they must have hit the gliders and as I said in that unit a lot of them went down.

Interviewer: *Fellows you knew*

Tom: *Fellows I knew, but obviously I had left some years before and the personnel had changed quite a bit but there would be quite a few of those who came down there I knew.*

Major Tom Howell

Figure 24 Tom Howell in Italy

Kings Road Depot continued as a Recruiting Centre throughout the War. Recruits were not exclusive to the RAMC. Private Henry Jones enlisted at the same time as Tom Howell in the summer of 1939 into 127 Field Ambulance. His younger brother, Leslie enlisted at Kings Road into the Royal Ordnance Corps. In 1941 he transferred to the RAMC and joined up with his brother, who had safely returned from Dunkirk with 146 Field Ambulance. Leslie took part in the airborne assault at Arnhem and was subsequently killed in action.[35]

The common heritage of the WW2 Manchester Medic is evident in the medals in the current Officers' Mess, with the African and Italian Star Medals identifying the areas in which many served. In the latter stages of the war the atrocities carried out by the Nazi Regime became apparent and one of 207's former Commanding Officers, Colonel Bob Price found himself as a young Medical Officer liberating Belsen Concentration Camp and attending to the sick and dying.

---

35 Leslie died on 13th April 1945 and is buried in Arnhem Oosterbeek war cemetery, grave reference 8.A.13

The lasting effect of war time experience was to remain with the men who served and those that chose to re-enlist when the TA was re-established in 1947. The WW2 legacy of highly experienced soldiers remained for several years. Their appreciation of large scale casualties made them ideal leaders in the preparation for "the Cold War". Lieutenant Colonel John Bennett sums up this hidden wealth of experience he encountered as a junior officer:

There was a lot of Regular experience – some of it war-time. Jack "the flag" Roberts had been mobilised during the Second World War and served as Company Commander at the military hospital in Davyhulme. It was often only at the Remembrance Day Parade when Service Dress with swords and medals were brought out that one realised. I remember in the spring of 1977 recounting how I had just seen the newly released film about Arnhem "A Bridge Too Far". John Mee muttered something about it had always been raining when he had to be out and about. He had been in the RAMC there. A quiet, unassuming man, he worked for Boots and was the Technical Quartermaster. He must have been one of the oldest Lieutenants in the Army List. Years later it was discovered that "paperwork had gone astray" and he was immediately promoted Major, with some (though not enough) antedate

John Mee's war record included service at Arnhem, after demobilisation the then Sergeant Mee re-joined the TA on its reformation in 1947. He survived several amalgamations, disbandments and reorganisations forming and retired in 1979, after more than forty years military service.

Figure 25 Warrant Officers' and Sergeants' Mess photographed outside the Kings Road building in 1948

This picture, which hangs today in the present Warrant Officers' and Sergeants' Mess, includes several members of 125 Field Ambulance who were with the unit when it joined the BEF in April 1940; QMS C Timperley (front rank, far left), Sgt T Taylor (centre rank, second from left), Sgt T Garratt (rear rank, second from left), Sgt J Shemerdine (centre rank, third from right). Several men mentioned in the last chapter are also in the picture; Jack "the flag" Roberts is sat in the front rank, third from right; John Mee is in the centre rank, far right and Tom Howell is sat fifth from the right on the front rank. The medal ribbons indicate that some of the men served in the Great War, and several are wearing oak leaves meaning they were mentioned in dispatches. Sergeant Harry Houghton (rear rank far left) was also awarded a Military Medal whilst attached the 12 Battalion the Parachute Regiment.

The Cold War

Interviewer: You mentioned you knew where you were going to be in Germany?
Maggie: We weren't supposed to know
Interviewer: You weren't supposed to know but did you?
Barry: Some of us were privileged enough to go on Operation 'Square Peg' where you went and inspected your 'MOBLOC': your Mobilisation Location, and as I said it was Hamm Girls School..... Everybody knew where we were going!
Major Maggie Bremner QARANC and Major Barry Ford RADC

Figure 26 Winsor Girls School, Hamm the 'secret' MOBLOC of 207 General Hospital in the event of World War 3 (printed by Kind permission of Kevin Moore ©2012)

The Cold War was a culmination of the tensions between two political ideologies, the Communist states of Russia and its allies and the democratic nations of the North Atlantic Treaty Organisation (NATO). The United Kingdom (UK) had a large commitment of armed forces based primarily in the north of West Germany, with extended lines of communication through Belgium to the coast and the ferry ports. At the highest point of deployment in the 1970's the British Army of the

Rhine totalled over 77,000 [40]. This large scale stand-off between the opposing forces concentrated and directed military doctrine.

NATO doctrine was one of offensive planning in anticipation of a Warsaw Pact breakout over the Teutoberger Wald heading towards the River Weser, where it would be engaged by a comparable NATO force. The medical casualty estimate involved planning to respond to this eventuality, a short, high casualty scenario with the possibility of tactical nuclear weapons being used. The Manchester General Hospital was one of the twelve General Hospitals that would be mobilised if such an event looked probable, heralding the start of World War Three. A General Hospital was expected to cater for up to 800 casualties. The TA hospitals were originally sited on the lines of communication and established similar working doctrines as the Casualty Clearing Stations of previous European campaigns. The advent of nuclear warfare required a departure from open canvas tentage to more protected brick buildings which were, in many cases, identified beforehand. If the building was big enough, tents were often erected inside to provide extra protection, and in the case of the German winter, extra warmth. 207 (Manchester) General Hospital was to be located in a large girl's school in Hamm near Munster. Senior Officers, as Major Ford has indicated, took the opportunity to visit their potential Mobilisation Location whilst on exercise in Germany. For the majority of the troops, Belgium and Germany were simply a bonus and part of being in the TA at that time:

At Munster we were billeted next to a school which was to be our true location if the Russians invaded. The barracks were filthy. We set up a tented hospital on the parade ground and I have an abiding memory of the CO changing his mind about where he wanted the HQ tent. He had the soldiers manhandling a fully erected tent up and down the parade ground for ages – amusing to watch.

At Leibenau we slept in disused German Army barracks allegedly once one of Hitler's 'Love Camps'. We went on a day trip to see the Communist Border and also the site of Belsen Concentration Camp. The RCT[36] Major, name of Edwards, got the convoy lost and had to ask the way!

Captain Mary Freeman

---

36 RCT Royal Corps of Transport now part of the Royal Logistical Corps

Figure 27 Stretford detachment drill team on the drill square at Lincoln Barracks, Munster, Germany 1988

The serious planning for such an eventuality provoked much thought and encapsulated many of the wider arguments of survivability from a nuclear war as Colonel Elder outlines:

People used to say to me, how many people d'you think will actually turn up, come the day? It used to worry us a lot you know, and you had it in the back of your mind the people that you'd ticked off as probably not appearing come the day………. One of the scenarios which I even then thought was daft was that we had to get these casualties back. The idea of this was a short war, it'd be all over in 11days and we would retain casualties in Germany until the war was over and you could take them on cross channel ferries back to the UK, and it was absolute codswallop. They said: "Oh the ferries wouldn't run, the trains wouldn't run". Can you imagine some railway worker in Manchester whose son is stuck in Calais because some railway worker wouldn't move them to Manchester, you know. It's just inconceivable, but this was the scenario: we would hold them in Germany because we couldn't evacuate them to the UK. The other thing was there would be no NHS beds. The NHS had no allocation of beds for these casualties and I thought come on: there's lads of ours being killed, maimed and wounded in

Germany and we can't find a bed for them in Wythenshawe[37], come on, you know, it does not make sense, but that was the scenario, that's what we were told would happen"

The TA had been reformed in 1947. The units present at Kings Road during this period were, 125, 126 and 127 Field Ambulances plus the Field Hygiene Platoon. The latter, as Major Alwyn Charlton describes, was a Brigade asset:

The platoon consisted of about twenty men, we had our own transport and we consisted mainly of men who had background into sanitation or water works

7th (Manchester) General Hospital and 12th Casualty Clearing Station used the Drill Hall at Norton Street from 1955 – 61 and moved into Kings Road when 126 Field Ambulance was amalgamated with 127. Elements of 126 went to another Field Ambulance in Bebbington on the Wirral. Other units also had a presence on the Kings Road site, notably the Royal Military Police who had a platoon based there for many years.

7th (Western) General Hospital (TA) gained the title 'Manchester' in 1953 and later the honour of wearing the Manchester Eagle emblem on their uniform (Appendix 2). By 1961 Casualty Clearing Stations had evolved into a role not dissimilar to those of General Hospitals and subsequently 12 CCS was merged with 7th (Manchester) General Hospital. In 1967 7th (Manchester) General Hospital (TA) was renamed 207 (Manchester) General Hospital RAMC (Volunteers) and the two remaining Field Ambulances (125 and 127) plus the Field Hygiene Platoon were disbanded and their staff absorbed into the General Hospital.

Many of the established medical officers served in more than one of the Manchester Units. Principal in this was Colonel George Steele who commanded 126 Field Ambulance (1959 –61) 127 Field Ambulance (1961 – 63), 7th (Manchester) General Hospital (1965 - 67) and became the first CO of 207 (Manchester) General Hospital in 1967. Also located on the Kings Road site from 1947 to 1967 was the Medical Administrative Department for 42 Infantry Brigade, including the office of Assistant Director of Medical Services.

---

37 Here Colonel Elder is referring to Wythenshawe Hospital now known as the University Hospital South Manchester

Figure 28 The Coates room of the Officer's Mess in 1962. From left to right; Colonel J F O'Grady TD, DL (Honorary Colonel 42nd Division 1947-49), Colonel J B Coates MC, Colonel R G W Ollerenshaw TD, QHS (CO 7th General Hospital 1957-60, Colonel J G S Holman MC (CO 7th General Hospital 1963-65), Colonel G A Steele TD, QHP, Colonel R Barraclough MBE, TD, QHS (ADMS 42nd Division 1962-67)

Initially the core group of Senior Non-Commissioned Officers (SNCO) and Officers within 207 (Manchester) General Hospital were soldiers who had served in WW2 or had done National Service. They provided a wealth of experience and a mature outlook as WO2 Mark Cecil explains:

> ……..*totally different because when they were doing National Service I think it was two choices, you went in the artillery or you became a chef. They all joined the artillery actually, but when they came out they joined the TA reservist as chefs, and obviously they had to go through a training program similar to what we did. It's the same kind of program, but theirs was a lot harsher because of the availability to turn round and say "Oi Nobby sort this out or I'll give you a slap". You can't do that nowadays with the progression of time.*

> *So they passed on their wisdom and knowledge to us, and because they started retiring and finishing from the 90s up to 2000, we lost a lot of good chefs though natural progression.*

As these individuals gradually retired, from the late 1970s, they gave way to a new generation of soldiers who were visualising and training for a war they hoped would never happen.

Figure 29 WO2 Mark Cecil in his field kitchen

The chance of mobilisation was slim as the legislation required to mobilise the TA on a collective basis stipulated a war scenario. Those who did volunteer to go had few employment rights. The role of the TA was questioned, not just on cost or its ability but also the more relaxed informality that was evident in many TA units of the era. The system was often described as two armies, Regular and TA.

> *We had a 800 bedded hospital and that's how we did our exercises and it was quite a colossal thing. When I joined you weren't so much aware of what your role was, you were glad to be a part of the military, which I was, and it's more of a family now more than people in the unit, and it's different to the Regular Army.*
>
> *Don't get me wrong, on the tours I've been on I've met a lot of people over the years that when I first met them they were either Lance Corporals, Corporals, Privates, Sergeants, Staff Sergeants and now some of them are Colonels, Lt Colonels, Commanders, CO's. But I think with the unit it's more a family thing and that's why when people – especially some, and I'll say that again, SOME regular soldiers think that the TA is a joke, and they have no idea how wrong they are. Because if it wasn't for people like us, volunteers the British Army would be very, very stretched, which they are now anyway.*

Sergeant Vinny March

The General Hospital was a large organisation, 800 beds, 36 wards, with all medical departments and administrative and logistical support. The extent of this organisational set up was invariably only seen on Exercise on the Continent when practising its war time role. "Petit Mash" Exercises were held in England, invariably at Saighton Camp, Chester, where large numbers of Army Cadets were used to mimic a mass casualty scenario.

This large organisation required a large number of individuals. Recruitment was extensive with the un-trained (medically) Combat Medical Technician being the main-stay of the establishment.

207, in keeping with the other TA hospitals, undertook a three year cycle of training on the Continent, commencing in 1970 by going to Rinteln in West Germany followed by three visits to Olen in Belgium (1973, 76, 79) back to Leibenau 1982 and finally to camps at Munster 1985 and 1988. These Camps were popular with the majority of soldiers attending. They proved invaluable for recruiting, often giving a young soldier their first experience of foreign travel. They also helped in the early years to shape and develop the corporate identity of a General Hospital:

Interviewer: Where is Olen?

Malcolm: Olen is south of Antwerp, on one of the main arterial routes into Germany. This was its main purpose in that it was a transit area and at the same time I believe there was a railhead there so our role as a General Hospital was to receive large amounts of casualties from the Ambulance Train.

Interviewer: This was the Cold War scenario.

Malcolm: That's right.

Interviewer: Did you get anywhere else other than Belgium?

Malcolm: Yes, we were on a three year cycle – so every three years we went close to what we might call our 'real' Cold War location. At that time in 1979, the Hospital was located in the rear but for the next annual camp, which was in Germany, at Leibenau 1982 we were moved into the forward area. The following two camps were at Lincoln Barracks in Munster, which I think was 1985 and 1988.

Captain Malcolm Jackson

Figure 30 Olen, Belgium - 207 General Hospital arriving on Annual Camp, 1976

Figure 31 On exercise in Belgium, the ambulance train arriving at the rail head in Olen, 1976

Figure 32 In this picture can be seen the then CO, Colonel Elder (on the right) and two future COs; Captain Gallagher (Stood with his hands behind his back) and Lieutenant Robertson (sat on the step)

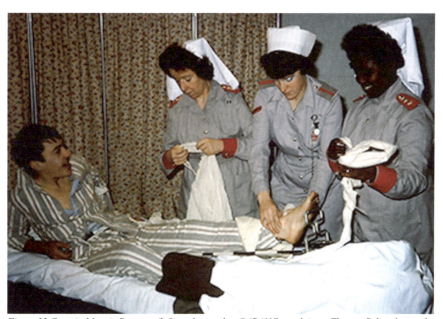

Figure 33 Captain Maggie Bremner (left) and two other QARANCs applying a Thomas Splint during the Olen exercise 1976

The Army Medical Services by the mid-1960s and into the 1970s were having to use training material largely left over from the Second World War, much of it becoming worn out and obsolete. The RAMC soldier thrived on assembling the hospital; they were tentage specialists, priding themselves on how quickly they could erect and pack away a hospital. This was a considerable logistical achievement given that many of the post war tents were heavy and bulky, such as "Tents Universal Assembly" had cast iron poles and spikes. All training equipment was kept in large storage depots throughout the UK, or as Sergeant Tommy Willis describes in similar depots based in West Germany with the British Army of the Rhine:

Interviewer: Did you take all your equipment with you? You were obviously on the Quartermasters staff.

Tommy: Yes I was always on the advance party when we went to these places. We took vehicles over with us. Any equipment we were short of we could pick up in Germany from a Regular unit..........

Interviewer: Where would you get your tents from?

Tommy: We would get them all from a Regular unit. I don't know if we took a certain amount of tentage with us but the bulk of it used to come from various units in the area. We took the basic trucks for taking the equipment and luggage and pick what they called pool vehicles up from somewhere over there.....

The last two Cold War camps were in Lincoln Barracks, Munster. It was a former German Infantry Barracks. Accommodation was in large blocks on various levels. Beer was very cheap and plentiful. As Captain Mary Freeman alludes to earlier, trying to place an 800 bed unit within the confines of a barrack square was very difficult and it kept the logistical support very busy taking down and erecting tentage. Sergeant Tom Slattery of the Royal Corps of Transport[38] with his JCB was probably the busiest man on camp. The main complex of the hospital was situated in the old stables, with the tentage extruding from the front. Accident and Emergency or rather Reception was at the front of the complex with an appropriate amount of space for the ambulance coaches, which were to be used in Germany, to turn around in. Evacuation was the other large hospital department with many of the wards dedicated to holding patients ready for

---
38 Now the Royal Logistical Corps

evacuation invariably via the hospital trains to the Belgian coast.

During the post war period the threat from the Warsaw Pact countries dominated, however, the UK was also engaged in other conflicts.

A group of six NCOs led by Staff Sergeant Bernard Furness and including Sergeant Tommy Willis went to Cyprus during the later stages of the uprising in 1959. No TA medical personnel went to the Falklands in 1982.

Northern Ireland was the main area of active deployment for the British Army during this period. The TA could not be mobilised for internal policing, but a few TA medics served there. The only "Manchester Medic" TA, was Corporal Andrew Higgins who was attached to the Royal Anglian Regiment for a six month tour in the mid-1990s.

The threat posed by the IRA to the UK mainland included attacks upon TA personnel, transport and bases. Heightened security brought about considerable change. Individuals were actively discouraged from wearing their uniform in public in case they attracted attention. Cars and unit transport were checked every time before use for bombs that may be attached. Railings and other security measures were erected to protect TA buildings including the HQ at Kings Road:

> *The IRA attacks on troops in Germany also considerably heightening the security situation. A suitcase left by its owner was considered a potential threat and was subsequently exploded on the drill square of Munster Barracks during the 1988 annual camp.*
>
> *Later on, whilst in BAOR 1988-90, shootings in Rheindahlen and on a cross-channel ferry forced the abandoning of British Forces Germany (BFG) vehicle licence plates and the elaborate "civilianising" of green military coaches used to ferry children around the many forces schools.*

Lieutenant Colonel John Bennett

The breakup of the Warsaw Pact and the Peace Accords signed with the USSR meant the beginning of a new world order. The nuclear age had passed; old enemies were soon to soldier side by side in peace time operations. The Balkans was to become the focus of nationalism trying to reassert itself on the European Continent. Civil war and genocide required new political and military responses; the Manchester Medic was soon to be found in Sarajevo, Pristina and other Balkan hotspots.

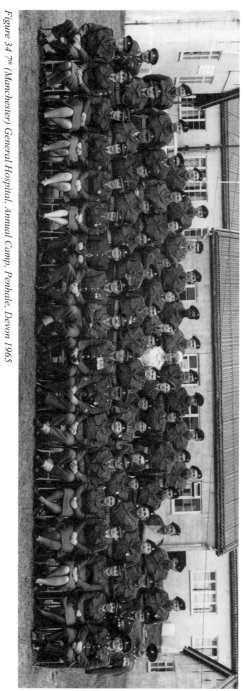

Figure 34 7th (Manchester) General Hospital, Annual Camp, Penhale, Devon 1965

First Gulf War 1990-1991, OPERATION (OP) GRANBY

The air raid sirens welcomed Corporal Andrew "Budgie" Burgess to King Khalid Airport in Saudi Arabia;

.....after that we all got on a double decker bus to be taken to our various camps, sitting for twenty minutes before our Regular (army) escort enquired could anyone drive a bus, it turned out we had 3 bus drivers amongst us. (only in the TA eh)

Iraq invaded and annexed Kuwait in August 1990. In response to this the United States of America (USA) and UK were asked to deploy armed forces to ensure the safety of Saudi Arabia. Initially RAF and Royal Navy personnel were deployed but eventually 7th Armoured Brigade from Germany was despatched. As the year went on an anticipated relief of staff became reinforcements for the forthcoming liberation of Kuwait. The TA and Reservists became a significant factor in these re-enforcements many being compulsorily mobilised. 205 (Scottish) General Hospital (Volunteers) were mobilised and had the honour of being the first TA Field Hospital to serve in combat since WW2. Shortfalls in their establishment and that of other medical facilities saw a significant number of 207 personnel mobilised throughout the world. The mobilisation process was to be refined over the forthcoming years as the TA became used more frequently. In the First Gulf war the process was fragmented and at times a lottery as the then Corporal March explains:

Interviewer: I think it's fair to say that the first Gulf was one of the first major deployments of TA personnel since the Second World War. You were part of that, what role did you play and how did that process go?

Vinny: Well what happened was a friend of mine, a young lady called Gwen Dwyer had put down to go for it, because you know, we'd had meeting and we'd been told that they required Medics.

Interviewer: You volunteered to do it?

Vinny: I volunteered to do it – at that time I didn't because, yea I was scared I'll be totally honest with you. But then, it was a freak accident, a friend of mine I'd talked into joining, and I worked *with her, and I think it was a Thursday, she'd been told her uniform was there and to pick it up but she didn't have a car. So I took her down in my car, and whilst she was getting her uniform I saw my friend Glen Dwyer in uniform. And I said to her "what are you doing here, what's going on? She told me that a couple of my other friends had gone, one being Andrew Burgess, who's now SSgt, and what she said to me was "it doesn't feel right if you're not there, it doesn't feel right" because we were a bit of a crew. So I went to see at the time I think it was a chap called Major Cass and asked him if I could go. He said if you're going to go, it's going to be tomorrow morning or not at all. So I had to make an on the spot decision, so I thought well yes I will do. So I did volunteer for it.*

The following day, we met at the unit, they took us down to Aldershot and we got processed. I got told when we were going, when we had to turn up, got given our – well we didn't get given any uniform because they didn't have any. I turned up at Saighton camp to start my training. It was split between Saighton camp and Sealand. I missed out on RAF Sealand by one person, because RAF Sealand was the better camp. We were attached to 205, who were at that time a General Hospital.

207 personnel were posted according to logistical need, though the majority were posted to 205 General Hospital based at Riyadh Airport in Saudi Arabia. Others were distributed between the more advanced Field Hospitals; some were further forward still being medics within the Armoured Brigade. The most unusual deployment was that of Captain Ian Lewin, a Radiographer who was mobilised to the Falkland Islands to enable the Regular radiographer to be posted back to his unit in the Gulf. Captain Lewin spent three months working and exploring the islands seeing penguins instead of camels.

The administrative process for TA and Reservists at this time was very primitive and one of the unfortunate problems to dog the mobilisation was poor logistical provision:

When I went out in 1991, we were sent to Aldershot first. We did this, we did that; mistakes were made obviously, admin instructions and what not. We got issued some kit, but not desert combats, so we had to go out there in "greens". At that time is wasn't like the uniform we wear now; we were wearing what we called moderate combat trousers, which were lined. We couldn't wear lightweights because that wasn't their role. Lightweights were just green trousers were there to do your menial tasks, and we didn't get issued kit until about six weeks in. We got promised everything and it was a joke to say: "Can we have this?" – "No, it's on the boat!" They flew us over, but all our equipment was on the boat.

Corporal Vincent "Vinny" March

Saddam Hussein, the Iraqi President, had used chemical weapons on his own people and had the capability to deliver them by missile. The Scud, a Russian missile, became a potent threat and preparations to combat its chemical threat became paramount even within medical facilities. Much of the pre-deployment training consisted of practising Nuclear, Bacteriological and Chemical (NBC) individual and collective drills for such an attack. These skills were quickly utilised once deployed as Corporal March explains:

Vinny: The Hospital was actually built in the half-finished King Khalid International Airport. We set up our hospital on the various floors and because it was only half completed there was a lot of dust, a lot of masonry, so we cleaned it all up and set up a COLPRO. Our first mission was to set up a COLPRO fully active.....

Interviewer: What was a COLPRO, what's it for?

Vinny: Well it's actually a hospital inside the Hospital. There were lots of threats of using nuclear or gasses – biological or nerve gas, there was always that threat. Every time it went dark, the sirens would go off and no matter where you were you had to stop, get under cover and put your respirator on. Everywhere you went you had your respirator with you.

Basically a COLPRO is a Collective Protective System. It's a big green tent that you put bits on to, just like your normal 18 x 24. All of this is called a forced air environment, air is filtered and pumped into this place, and it can be any size..... If we lost power obviously the actual COLPRO would start going down like a balloon. In the operating theatre we put an 18 x 24 frame (which was my idea) so if it did go down at least you wouldn't have a tent on top of a patient on the table!

> *I worked with a chap called Ollie Stonehouse. He was the Warrant Officer, and he adopted me for the first 4 weeks as we were building this COLPRO. Because, as you know, you get one design, we'd put it up and somebody would come along, an officer most of the time: "Oh I didn't want that there, I want that there, I want this here, I want that here". So you had to totally change it all round.*
>
> *And then another point that I brought up was that the COLPRO was right next to big glass windows and opposite the airport was a mosque, and I said if anything was to land within half a mile all this glass would get shattered and you'll have a Swiss cheese. We erected blast curtains alongside where the COLPRO was; it was about a good 40 – 50 feet long.*

The daily television coverage of events raised the concern level of families left behind in England. The indiscriminate use of Scuds meant that even troops in the rear areas were potentially vulnerable. To ease the families concerns a video of 207 personnel taken on deployment, a piece of new technology in 1990, was screened at HQ.

Once deployed, the TA, Reservists and Regulars had to work together often in a grim desert environment which was unseasonably, wet and cold. Most 207 personnel were positive about their deployment and working with Regular Troops. The resulting Ground War was quickly concluded, enabling most TA personnel to arrive back un-harmed and safe in February – March 1991:

> *In all, we were away for three months, all attached personnel came back a couple of weeks after 205, not to a civic reception but to a PSI who was upset at having to give up his day off to come and pick us up.*
>
> Corporal Andrew Burgess

As the crowds spilled over onto the Berlin Wall, jubilation at the dawning of a new world order shifted the context of the armed forces. A successful Gulf Campaign did not spare the armed services from drastic cuts in manpower. Many lessons had been learned from the First Gulf War, particularly about the efficiency of mobilising TA and Reservists. Options for Change (1991) saw considerable down-sizing in the Army. A more robust usage of the TA was seen as a practical use of resources. Concerns over job security and status whilst serving had to be addressed as did the Services' desire that certain groups and individuals, if required, could be compulsory mobilised to fill key positions, a considerable factor in the new specialised Army Medical Services. The 1996 Reserve Forces Act enshrined most of the key concerns and objectives becoming the benchmark Act as to the role of the individual and the collective TA.

During the late 1980s and 1990s, the Conservative Governments of Margaret Thatcher and John Major wanted all governmental organisations to be managerially and financially sound, providing value for money and not over-burdening the tax payer. The post-Cold War era made it inevitable that significant reorganisation would happen. The brunt of reductions was experienced within the infantry. The Regular Medical services saw the closure of many of the Military Hospitals. The Army lost The Duchess of Kent Military Hospital at Catterick, The Cambridge Military Hospital at Aldershot and The Queen Elizabeth Military Hospital in Woolwich, London. The RAF Hospitals at Wroughton and Ely eventually closed, and the Naval Hospital Haslar at Gosport was considerably reduced in size. All of the British Military Hospitals abroad were also closed during this time, with the exception of Gibraltar and Cyprus. Millbank, the home of the RAMC was to be sold, and Keogh barracks the long established depot for generations of RAMC soldiers and officers became a Tri-service establishment.

Options for Change over saw the re-organisation of major parts of the Army in attempts to streamline and make it capable of meeting future anticipated needs.

The Adjutant General's Corps (AGC) was established, combining many of the Hospital's non-medical staff including all clerks. The chefs left the Catering Corps and were re-badged into the newly-created Royal Logistic Corps.

It was also the era of sexual equality: the Woman's Royal Army Corps was disbanded and their serving soldiers were incorporated in the appropriate cap badge with many being absorbed into the AGC. Male nurses who were previously RAMC were to be re-badged to the Queen Alexandra's Royal Army Nursing Corps (QARANC). For many this proved to be a contentious proposition, particularly for individuals who had served for many years as RAMC. Major Paddy Dwyer was

Figure 35 Major Paddy Dwyer (front) and Captain Atwal explaining to Prince Philip, Duke of Edinburgh how patients are tracked around the hospital during his visit to the Kings Road Depot in 1999

the last 207 RAMC Nursing Officer to bow out gracefully. Prior to joining the TA, he had a distinguished military career, serving as a Regular Officer in Northern Ireland and the Gulf.

207 (Manchester) Field Hospital (Volunteers) was formed in 1993, with Colonel Paddy Gallagher becoming the Commanding Officer. The letters: RAMC were dropped from the title, reflecting the wide range of medical professionals required to run an operational Field Hospital. Mobility, not static beds became the key factor as the Field Hospitals were required to hold only 200 patients. Fewer beds meant fewer staff; the medically untrained CMTs took the brunt of the man power cuts.

Options for Change also had an impact locally: in 1992 the unit lost Detachments in Lancaster and Macclesfield, considerably reducing the recruitment catchment area.

Detachments at Ashton-Under-Lyne and Stockport were added in 1995, along with a significant number of ex – Fusiliers. Bury was added in 1997. The suffix: "Detachment" was replaced with "Squadron", recognising the more mobile element of a Field Hospital. 207 (Manchester) Field Hospital (Volunteers) now comprised:

'A' Squadron at Ashton and Stockport
'B' Squadron at Blackburn
'C' Squadron and HQ Squadron at Kings Road Manchester.
'G' Squadron at the Castle Armoury Bury.

Figure 36 OP GRANBY 1991, aerial photograph of 32 Field Hospital taken from a landing Puma Helicopter

We were formed from BMH Hannover, but were a hotpotch of personnel from 59 different units, including all 3 services, the TA and Reservists. It is astonishing that from such disparate origins we could achieve so much, so quickly. But it was just as well that we did for we had to deal with most of the casualties.

Colonel Peter Lynch, Commanding Officer of 32 Field Hospital. Extracted from the speech he gave on the morning the Unit ceased to exist (21 March 1991). Three members of 207 served with this unit.

People and places

.....I knew that our RHQ building was one of the very first TA units in Manchester, which again is something to be proud of. When I got into the Sergeants' mess, we had a picture, an old black and white picture of all the senior ranks plus their CO, 2IC, and their Adjutant and so on, all sitting cross-legged in front of the unit doors. I think it was 1948. 'Jack the Flag'[39] was a Warrant Officer at the time, (because I think he was a retired Major), and what we actually did was recreated that picture but with the modern day soldiers. It turned out that one of the chaps, I think it was one of the officers that was on the picture, was still alive. We invited him down to the unit. He was so overwhelmed when he saw that we done an exact replica picture, set out exactly the same way.

A little bit of accidental history: I remember when we were getting the Drill Hall done up for the first time, and it got stripped down, there was something actually written on the wall near what's now the Sergeants' Mess, I can't remember what it was, it wasn't 252, but was like 155 or 254 whatever number it was, medical hospital[40].

Sergeant Vincent 'Vinny' March RAMC

The Kings Road site has seen considerable usage over the one hundred years since its construction. Volunteers from the Great War onwards have left through this building on their way to conflicts and wars. The medical units and the vast numbers of volunteers have also required additional resources in terms of buildings, primarily hospitals and training establishments. 207's ancestors had close affiliations with many of the region's major hospitals, primarily Manchester Royal Infirmary (MRI). Many beds in local hospitals were taken over by the military during both World Wars. Other facilities such as schools and large psychiatric hospitals were also utilised. The War Memorial by the art gallery at the end of Greek Street, Stockport stands on the

---

39 'Jack the Flag' was the 'affectionate' term used by members of the unit to refer to Major Jack Roberts. He joined the unit prior to WW2 as a private, rising to the rank of Brevet Major, and retired in 1979 (he never really left!!).
40 Other anecdotal evidence suggests that this sign gave directions to one of the Field Ambulances. There were also markings on the wall that indicated that a stair well had been there.

site of a former school which was used as a military hospital during the Great War. The 5th (Western) General Hospital, the predecessor of the 7th (Manchester) General Hospital, was established at Park Hospital, Davyhulme (now Trafford General Hospital) during WW2.

During the course of both World Wars not all of the medical volunteers served abroad, many saw service in the North West of England caring for the large volume of casualties received from the fighting front. Not all casualties were from direct action, the flu pandemic of 1917 –18 was to account for considerable numbers of medical staff, including a number of the female nurses and VAD mentioned on the memorial at Kings Road who were working in local hospitals.

The rehabilitative care developed in local hospitals is still evident today, notably the Manchester Disablement Services Centre now part of the University Hospital South Manchester which can trace its beginnings to the Great War.

The Army reorganisation following the Haldane Report of 1907 was based upon local or district Divisions. The East Lancashire Division that was to become 42nd Division, became the regional infantry fighting force to which medical units were administratively attached. This arrangement remained in place during both World Wars. The requirement for suitably trained volunteers saw the establishment of detachments (or latterly squadrons) being formed throughout Lancashire and Cheshire. The mill towns of Rochdale, Burnley and Bury were major recruiting grounds for soldiers in World War One and were to suffer many of the losses recorded on the Great War memorial at Kings Road.

The Second World War witnessed changes in recruiting and how staff were utilised. Manchester had always provided three Field Ambulances and a General Hospital. Following Dunkirk many experienced staff were placed throughout the Army to provide the nucleus of newly established medical units.

The amalgamation of all the medical units in 1967 achieved the aim of concentrating resources in buildings, people and administrative functioning into one HQ within a designated geographical location: Kings Road. The unit's identity is firmly based within the context of Manchester. The Manchester Eagle forms part of the cities heraldry and in 1959 the unit was honoured by the city and allowed to wear this emblem on their uniform.

Figure 37 Still worn with pride – The Manchester Eagle

In the last forty years, cuts in the armed forces have left the present Field Hospital as the only Medical Unit in Greater Manchester. The reduction that has taken place has mirrored the present domestic and international political requirements of maintaining a standing Army. Although the number of individuals required to fill the medical establishment has reduced, the number of outlying Detachments has remained historically the same, Kings Road plus three others, presently we have four other squadrons locations based at Ashton–Under–Lyne, Bury, Stockport and Blackburn This decentralisation allows for a large geographical recruiting area with the objective to spread the recruiting net further to get the trained and qualified staff now required with possible deployment a significant factor.

Interviewer: *Alan how long have you been in the unit?*

Alan: *Coming up to 24 years now. I originally came down, not necessarily to join the medical corps; it was my local TA centre as such, to find out about the Reserve Forces in general. Once I'd been interviewed, the rest is history. I was signed up for the laboratory....*

Interviewer: *....so you didn't necessarily sign up for that, you* *actually joined up to be a soldier?*

Alan: *Well, no, it was basically an information-gathering evening at my local TA centre. It turned out more or less: "You're going in for a commission, sign here and off you go!"*

Interviewer: *So they got you on the first go?*

Alan: *Yes. The next thing I knew it was a commissioning board at Fulwood, Preston and my initial appointment was as a Second Lieutenant, so I have gone from Mister to Major in that period of time....*

Major Alan McKinnon RAMC

Drill Halls were invariably placed within the centre of communities. Recruitment came from the predominantly male working population whose hours and terms of employment required easy access and within walking distance in an era largely dependent on public transport. Within a mile radius of the Kings Road we still have two TA centres. Major Tom Howell gives an insight to the other military establishments locally prior to WW2:

Tom: *....well there were outbuildings for the QM stores right at the back.*

Interviewer: *Was the car park there?*

Tom: *Yes but that wasn't available to us. I think that belonged to the Post Office at that time, or the Signals. There was a Signals Barracks where the Post Office buildings are. Bob Ollerenshaw, a past ADMS, started in the Signals.*

Interviewer: *I never knew that – so all that ground technically was all military at one time.*

Tom: *Yes the whole area. The Duke of Lancs were just up Upper Chorlton Road on the left, and the RASC on the top left, up towards the pub[41], It was like a little military enclave then.*

Major Tom Howell RAMC

Many came straight from work, so a cooked meal and refreshments

---

41 The pub referred to here is the Seymour that stood at the junction of Upper Cholton Road and Manchester Road until the turn of the 21st Century. The RASC building still remained as a TA barracks.

were provided to help ensure attendance. Historically all medical units based in Manchester have had outlying detachments. Bury, Rochdale, Burnley to name just a few, have at one time provided medical volunteers. Drill training nights before 1967 were on a Tuesday and Thursday nights. Following the 1967 amalgamation, a Detachment was established at Blackburn, and proved very successful. Colonel Elder gives an insight into the decision to expand and establish a new Detachment in an untested area, Cheshire:

Interviewer: Why Macclesfield?

Bill: Well, we decided that we had a few people who came from round there: Congleton, Macclesfield, that southern end of the patch, and we thought: "We'll get them to attend, but at Macclesfield" and then we'll see if we can recruit there because it had supported a whole battalion from the Cheshire Regiment at one time. TAVRA[42]

---

42 What is TAVRA: Territorial Army and Volunteer Reserve Association

Figure 38 Colonel J B Coates MC opening Lancaster detachment

said to me: "Better units than yours have tried and failed" and I thought: "Right, I'll show 'em!", and we did. We got a Detachment going and, this stood me in good stead when I went to start one at Lancaster, because I'd a track record of starting detachments, and so, we got the go ahead to Lancaster against a lot of opposition from the Queens Lancashire Regiment. They wouldn't let us in their Drill Hall but we got a hut in Halton Camp and that was very good. And we had JB Coates, son of Sir William Coates to come and open it.....
Colonel Bill Elder RAMC

As Detachments were added, the Permanent Staff Instructors (PSI) could not provide support as there were only two of them, so Drill Nights were staggered. Tuesday at Stretford, Wednesday at Blackburn, Thursday at Macclesfield and Lancaster, with the PSIs taking it in turn to visit the Detachments. This arrangement also meant that individuals could attend Stretford on Tuesday to collect clothing or do administrative duties and attend their own Detachment later in the week.

The Detachments thrived, with both Macclesfield and Lancaster getting new purpose built TA centres to replace the old buildings, however, in 1992, a decision was made to reduce 207's recruiting profile and both these new centres were taken over by 208 Field Hospital Liverpool.

The later part of 2009 saw nearly all TA training suddenly cancelled and although this decision was later reversed the pressure to save money due to the growing financial crisis had inevitable consequences. As Major Alison Diskin describes;

In the latter part of 2009, an eerie silence fell upon Canterbury Street Barracks as the Government's plans to cut £20 million from the TA's budget hit home and training was kept to a bare minimum. Footsteps echo in what was once a busy drill hall. Even when the unpopular decision was reversed it was clear that there was little hope that the barracks would survive and by the end of the year rumours abounded about its fate.

I took over command of B Squadron in November of that year and fought desperately on behalf of the Blackburn detachment to save what had been its home since the sixties, but the inevitable happened, and closure was announced. There was a real sense of sadness felt by those who had trained there for many years. Not only at the loss of a wonderful building, steeped in history, but at the disbandment of 93 Signal Squadron, with whom B Squadron had shared the barracks and a close working relationship for decades.

Figure 39 Blackburn Detachment at Canterbury Street in the 1990s

Figure 40 Members of B Squadron (Blackburn) OP TELIC 4a 2004

It was in March 2010 that the door to Canterbury Street Barracks was closed and the key turned for the final time, before the short journey across Blackburn to B Squadron's new home. Somme Barracks, already occupied by the 4th Battalion, the Duke of Lancaster's Regiment, is a modern building, with excellent facilities. It was ironic that that first thing that greeted B Squadron was a poignant old photograph of hundreds of soldiers, with anxious faces, outside Canterbury Street Barracks, waiting to be moved out to the Front during the First World War. I wonder what they would make of the bulldozers and demolition of their once home?

Buildings

The Kings Road premises have physically evolved in size and areas of usage over many years. Following the 1967 amalgamation and another change in role, Chef Sergeant Steve Randall describes the set up in early 1970's:

Steve: *When I first joined, the kitchen is now where it was then, but every room on the bottom floor was to do with the kitchen, kitchen stores and everything like that. Up the steps were the toilets and the MI[43] room. Back from there, it was one big open Drill Hall. There was no partition or false ceiling, it went right up to the eaves, and right to the back door and they just had wagons and Land Rovers and everything else in there. There was the old Nissen hut at the back, the Romney hut what we call now the G10 store.*

Sergeant Steve Randall

Staff Sergeant Tommy Willis remembers other aspects:

Tommy: *The RMPs (Royal Military Police) were up where the Admin Offices used to be, on the 1st floor opposite the Officers' Mess. The building has been knocked about a lot and shortened, the garages and all that, because it was a big Drill Hall then.*

Interviewer: *Did you come in through the front door off the street or did you come in through the garage?*

Tommy: *Yes, the front door was always open*

Interviewer: *Did you have a guard on it?*

---

43 MI room – Medical Inspection room

Figure 41 First Aid training in the Kings Road drill hall in the 1960s

Tommy: *Yes, there was security on the door*

Interviewer: *Was that to make sure you didn't get out or that you got in?*

Tommy: *A bit of both, joking apart, it was to vet who was coming in, because anybody could just walk through the door.*

Staff Sergeant Thomas "Tommy" Willis

During the late 70s security throughout the Armed Forces was increased to reflect the growing threat from the Provisional Irish Republican Army (PIRA).

The security system was very variable in the seventies and eighties. Uniform was openly worn, despite IRA attacks on the mainland. There seemed to be little logic in our response. I did a student elective in Aldershot in 1978, not long after a bomb had exploded at The Parachute Regiment depot there, killing a Roman Catholic padre. Despite this, buildings and their grounds were relatively open even when I returned in 1984. Major Kim Stevens, surgical registrar, used to cycle in to work wearing his para beret.
Lieutenant Colonel John Bennett

The IRA security threat of the 1980s eventually saw TA units go behind security fences away from the local population. The old Macclesfield Drill Hall on Bridge Street was probably one of the last to accept visitors straight from the street with only a very large Corporal Geoff Ashmore standing in the way. This enforced division from the community and further security reviews, which have seen the once constant use of the drill hall facilities decline, has to a large account further alienated the military from their local community which were the source of recruiting.

Figure 42 The Kings Road depot in 1960 at the time it also served as the Manchester Garrison Medical Centre (Courtesy of Manchester Libraries, Information and Archive, Manchester City Council)

Recruits and Training

The reasons for enlisting during peace time differ significantly from those seen during a national crisis.

The character and attributes of a volunteer are significantly different from individuals who join up for regular service. Certain individuals have always joined the TA to see if they suit military life and if it is agreeable go on to join the Regulars.

The TA soldier is invariably older than his Regular counterpart. With age comes maturity, the individual often having a family, profession or career. The ability to commit time to the TA is the major factor in both recruitment and retention. Paid soldiering is a significant inducement, particularly in times of economic hardship but cannot be placed against the wrath of a neglected spouse, and has to be viewed against a history of volunteers paying to enlist and buy their own uniforms. Recruits from the Regular Army, those generally who have enjoyed the military system and wish to continue beyond their 22 years, form a small but significant number.

Increasing demands for trained soldiers are coupled with the desire of the soldier to get something for themselves out of the Army. Shooting, adventurous pursuits, civilian qualifications or foreign travel, to name a few, play an important part in retaining the individual and by offering them something unique and interesting, a fine balance is struck between employer, the military and the soldier.

Figure 43 From left to right, Majors Robert (Bob) Jordon, Colin Gidman and Rodger Sharpe. All ex-regular RSMs of the RAMC

Recruiting during peacetime can present significant

problems as there are many alternatives that may appear as attractive. Word of mouth remains the most potent method of recruiting, and implies a local or communal association with existing members, as Sergeant Vinny March explains:

....as a cadet I didn't really know that the TA existed. I got to know a few people; they told me where the unit was and at the time, from where I lived, it was 5 minute walk.

I think after about another year I then came to 207. I liked what I saw. I didn't know that you got paid because in the Cadets you only got paid for your uniform and so on and so forth, so I thought I'd give it a shot. It was just to get into another military establishment because I was getting too old for the Cadets at that time. I came here, liked what I saw, a few of the people that I met on that weekend were here[44], and I felt very welcome. I originally joined in 1982. After about 9 months, I actually joined the Regular Army: the Parachute Regiment. Unfortunately I dislocated my right shoulder, so that was that finished. A good friend of mine, Chris Dorrington who was a PSI here at the time talked me into coming back, which I did in 1985, and I've been here ever since.

Effective and imaginative training, providing opportunities that cannot be found elsewhere are again assets to recruiting. Colonel Elder explains the concept of good training and a positive image:

.....as a TA Officer I became the training officer, so I had to write a training programme. This took a long time because we had to write out a training programme for soldiers and then we had to write out a training programme for Officers. Two or three of us got together and wrote out these training manuals and training programmes. In the TA, there was a cycle of training, independent of medical units: individual training, collective training, collective training in BAOR and so on, (if it was a BAOR roled unit). The training programme, particularly in the TA which had Regular Training Officers, was virtually the same every year, so one was an NBC weekend, a drill weekend, a weapon weekend and so on. Now the excuse for this, particularly with a regular CO, was that they had to reach certain objectives, certain aims. But of course the recruit

---

44 Vinny was a cadet in the early 1980s and played a casualty during exercise 'Green Octopus' where he first encountered 207 (Manchester) General Hospital RAMC(V).

from the TA could find it boring. He knew every March he was going to be NBC, every April it was going to be something else and within a year or two they'd lost interest and left. So the turn-over in the TA even now is bad and certainly was bad then and I blame this on this lack of imaginative training. So we gave people objectives, tried to encourage people to attend, to meet these objectives, and, and make this unit a better unit with a lot of basic things – uniforms, dress, drills. All that sort of thing all counted towards making it better. We had a shooting team which won prizes, this sort of thing. So we had to improve the image of the unit right across the board.

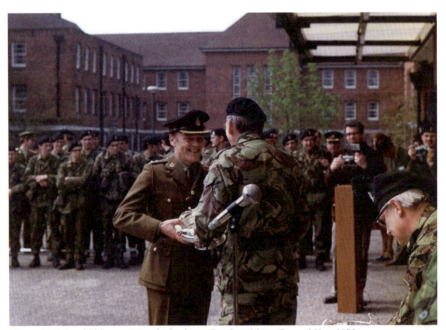

Figure 44 Colonel Elder receiving the Lucknow Cup from Major General Hart 1978

General Hospitals were very labour intensive, Combat Medical Technicians (CMT) forming the bulk of the man power invariably doing most of the heavy non-medical work as well as specified medical roles.

Interviewer: *How big was this organisation in 1976?*

Steve: *We were definitely up to about 200 strong.*

Interviewer: *Did you train at Stretford?*

Steve: *Yes on a Tuesday night, at least 80 people going about their business, because the drill hall was a big drill hall and not as you see it now as small offices.*

Sergeant Steve Randall

These large numbers were better represented on annual camp and major medical exercises as Sergeant Cecil describes

I remember at Westdown Camp, Steve and I were on the night shift and we had the laundry platoon who used to do all the laundry for the hospital. Those guys came in and washed pots for us. I was sat about 5 pallets high on top of compo boxes and we must of been doing about 5 or 600 meals, three times a day throughout the hospital complex and it was 100% compo, and obviously we had to sort the menus out. So all that compo that needed opening and we only had 2 can openers.

The CMTs were predominantly the untrained medical workers whose initial responsibility, when mobilised, would be the building of a large tented hospital and the installation of all equipment including beds. The need to recruit and retain large numbers was a constant battle.

Figure 45 The Laundry Platoon. These units were independent of the hospital and were cap badged Royal Army Ordnance Corps, Olen, 1976

Major General T Hart came to congratulate the unit in January 1980 on:-

> "being the first TA General Hospital to achieve 100 per cent recruitment since the Second World War.... Nineteen year old Private Eric Rawson from Ploughbank Road, Chorlton-cum-Hardy was the recruit whose attestation made him the 100 per - center!"
>
> Journal of the Royal Army Medical Corps 1980, page 55

The dilemma facing any Government is the cost of paying for a large Reservist force yet still getting value for money

> ...... the Territorial Army is currently held at low readiness against the possibility of a Cold War threat - to defend against an invasion, primarily by the Soviet Union, and Spetsnaz attacks on vital installations in the United Kingdom. Part of the judgment in determining that readiness level was that, understandably, the Government would resort to compulsory call-out of the Territorial Army only in the most extreme circumstances. However, that begs the question of what to do if the possibility of such circumstances arising becomes so remote that we do not have to maintain any standing forces against them. [41]

This questioning has gone on throughout the history of the TA and the Militia before questioning the usage of the TA, and producing a feeling of political inertia at times towards the TA. George Robertson MP, the then Defence Secretary, epitomised the view at the end of the Cold War of: "We have them, what do we do with them?", or "ignore them until we need them". The recent conflict in Iraq, and currently in Afghanistan demonstrates a definite need for the TA, the TA medic in particular, and a desire to include the TA and Reservists as equal and valued partners with the Regular Army: the "One Army" concept. To ensure that this parity is achieved, training (as mobilisation is a real probability) has now to be focused to ensure that both the unit and the individual are capable of successfully undertaking any mission they may go on in the future.

Training at home and abroad

> The whole ethos I think of the TA, I think anyway, is this sense of fun. If you lose that sense of fun there's no point being in it any more. For me, I spent 40 years in the TA and the Regular Army

and for me it was a hobby and I used to liken it to playing golf. I'll never be a professional golfer, but I'd like to be able to play golf well enough to compete with my contempories or even with a professional. I don't regard myself, and never will regard myself as professional golfer or a professional soldier 'cos I'm not, you know......

Colonel Bill Elder

Figure 46 On exercise in Gibraltar 2001

The TA training role is to enable volunteers to practice military skills to a level that enables them to provide assistance and support to the Regular Army. This objective has been retained since the formation of the TA. For the TA soldier, training takes place on a night at their local Drill Hall, at a weekend at a regional training venue and on an Annual Camp where they are expected to serve for 15 consecutive days. The list of Annual Camps (Appendix 4) undertaken by 207, illustrates the history and function of the unit over the last forty years. Either as a General or Field Hospital the training has been directed by the Commanding Officer and when required tasks carried out for various parts of the military organisation. The training mirrors the perceived role of the Army at that particular time and how the medical services would support them. Training prior to the Great War involved transporting men and materials by horse, route marches and exercises in support of the infantry, mainly on Salisbury Plain. The emphasis was on the management and movement of large volumes of casualties. WW2 training was more mobile and technical, in keeping with the manoeuvrist approach. Large amounts of casualties were again expected, and the clinical training was broad and generalist, rudimentary First Aid, aimed at transporting individuals quickly to treatment areas. The Cold War scenario of large scale casualties from a highly mobile force and the possibility of nuclear attack, dictated the post war training until the late 1990s. Medical training in the 21st Century, with the increased probability of mobilisation, sees the TA medical services in support of a smaller more robust Army, but forming the majority of the medical units available. This smaller unit is better trained in terms of clinical role and civilian experience, and is expected to function for months at a time rather than an entire war episode. Individuals rather than the hospital per se are the valued commodity, as the TA has learnt to manage an increasingly smaller pool of qualified individuals.

When medical staff are recruited, they are required to become soldiers, to familiarise themselves in a military role, function and procedures. This is an essential insight, as the volunteer aims to be professional but not to take on the identity of a Regular soldier as Colonel Elder succinctly describes. An annual Bounty is paid to all TA soldiers who complete specific training tasks. These set tasks are not medical (though there is a basic First Aid test) but are designed to show a basic standard of soldiering. For non-medical staff, becoming part of the Army Medical Services will require specific training. The Medical Orderly, Company Medic, Medical Assistant, Combat Medical Technician or the variety of other identities taken on board by the untrained soldier over the past one hundred years, have required specific Corps training, outlining their basic role and responsibilities before they go onto more specialised roles as medical stores personnel or Ward Masters.

> *I joined in October 1981 as 24467841 Private Rowland in the role of a Medical Assistant or MA for short. This role was given to those people who joined 207 General Hospital as it was then, who didn't have any professional medical training but wanted to be a medic. In those days the training wasn't as technical as it is today, for example your MA Class 3 would be trained to the level of a St John's First Aider.*

Major Charles Rowland RAMC

Figure 47 Macclesfield Detachment, winners of the 1985 drill competition, Munster. Holding the shield is the then Corporal Charles Rowland

It is not just medical staff who have to be trained, clerks, drivers and chefs have their own career pathways to enable them to be functioning individuals supporting the effective running of the Hospital.

Interviewer: How were you trained up to be a chef then, because obviously you came here to be an electrician?

Steve: To start with you stand by the chefs who were in there and learn by somebody showing you how to chop this and make that. If you wanted to learn the pastries you go into the pastry kitchen. Fortunately we had two excellent chefs who were good at pastries and did nothing else. Sergeant Sharman and Staff Vernon were brilliant at the pastry side of it, so if you wanted to learn that, that's where they'd put you. We never bought anything in cooked. We'd make all our own, right down to the basic gateaux; everything was cooked recipe-perfect from the manuals.

We had twenty-one chefs in the unit and you'd go away on your training courses. I did mine in Preston, at Fulwood Barracks that *is where I learnt to do my basic chef stuff with a few sauces and gravies'. The majority you learnt back in your unit by going away on weekends. They give you a little bit more to do, a bit of pastry, a bit more meat, put you on the savouries, and it's a learning factor because they can't waste the food. It's not like, where you can pretend to have patients. When we're on exercise we're actually doing it for everybody.*

My first camp, I fractured my arm about two weeks before we were going out to Belgium, so I thought I wasn't going. They told me: "If you break your legs you're still going, we're going to carry you there!", so with a Plaster of Paris on my arm they took me to Belgium. By the end of the first week I'd broke the plaster and it was straight to carrying things in the kitchen. It was a great Camp.

Sergeant Steve Randall

Medical training in its duration, intensity and knowledge required has varied over the century and mirrors the envisaged role on deployment, as Tom Howell describes from WW2:

Tom: *We got lectures on the bones of the body, muscles and things like that – it went on from that to First Aid training – and then inevitably that led to the Thomas Splint – which ultimately you did in the dark – and then the contents of FMP 1 and FMP2 – Field Medical Pannier 1 and 2. You got to know all the locations of everything in those, so if you are operating in the dark, when no lights were allowed, you knew exactly where to go.*

One of the personal goals set by many TA volunteers is about self-achievement, doing something special. For a TA medic, going through prolonged and at times mentally demanding training, with the possibility at some time that an individual's life may depend on your skills, can be very rewarding and a source of personal pride and achievement :

Martin: *One of the best compliments I ever had was from a civi nurse out in Gulf and he turned round and said: "I can't believe somebody wants to learn so much stuff in such a short time!" He taught me a lot and in the end I actually went and taught Regulars how to do ECGs, two weeks after me doing the thing for the first time and I thought: "Well, that's great and now I learned something* *and I've pressurised myself into doing that and that's part of the beauty about being a medic I think".*

Interviewer: *So can you remember the early days of your medical training, where was that done for instance?*

Martin: *Medical training was done at Saighton camp in Chester a lot of the time. Everybody loved going there because it was nearby....... The CMT's would have lessons from the nurses. Sometimes the doctors would teach and we were just sat there like "ERR what's he talking about now?"*

Corporal Martin Clarey

The Hospital has always trained its own staff. The Army Medical Services provide core training, with individuals going to depots for basic and more advanced training. The main training centre at present is Keogh Barracks near Aldershot, for many years the spiritual home of the RAMC having seen many generations of medics pass through.

For the medical volunteer who already has civilian qualifications, becoming a soldier and being familiar with the equipment is more of a concern. For many though, encompassing the TA spirit and the desire to assimilate into a military environment on a part-time basis was the attraction and maintained their interest as the then Corporal Malcolm Jackson explains:

Malcolm: *My main interest in life is shooting. One of the attractions of the Army was that there were weapons that I couldn't get my hands on normally, such as the Stirling sub-machine gun, and you could take these out on the ranges. So, to actually get a nice sunny day out on the ranges, which is what I pay for in civilian life, getting paid for it was fantastic.*

Interviewer: *Over those years you must have come across a variety of equipment and munitions.*

Malcolm: *Yea we would mainly use the Browning 9 mm pistol, the Self Loading Rifle (SLR), or the Stirling Sub machine gun. If we were lucky, we'd borrow a gimpy[45] and a few links and have a crack at it on the ranges.*

---

45 Gimpy – General purpose machine gun

Chemical Biological Radiological and Nuclear (CBRN) training is the present manifestation of training in response to man-made industrialised attack. Generations of soldiers have endured the "gas chamber", and running around in "Noddy Suites" to gain an appreciation of the debilitating effects of protecting oneself in response to a CBRN threat. The gas attacks during the Great War saw the introduction of the rudimentary gas mask. The protective, charcoals suits were introduced to give protection in a nuclear age, thankfully they were never used in that capacity but were worn on active service in desert conditions during both Gulf Wars.

Major David Asher relives his experiences of CBRN testing then known as NBC testing:

"It's your turn now; off you go, into the gas chamber". We put on our NBC suits, commonly known as 'Noddy Suits'. These consisted of baggy trousers and a hooded anorak-type top. There were special boots and gloves and the whole ensemble was completed by a gas-mask or respirator, as it is more correctly known. This had to be fitted correctly and there were different sizes according to your head size. We were expected to be able to don the mask in nine seconds from the order: "Gas; gas; gas!" being given (Why Nine seconds? Why not eight or ten?). One of the instructors would then come round checking you were correctly dressed in your 'Noddy Suit' and then wafted around the edges of the mask a wad of cotton wool soaked in something volatile like ether to test if there were any leaks. When the instructors were satisfied that everyone was safe to enter the chamber, the order was given to detonate a small canister of tear gas in the chamber, usually a small brick building built for the purpose. We lined up just outside the entrance door. This opened and we were led in. Visibility inside was poor partly because of the mask and also because the gas was steam-like in appearance. We walked around in single file for a few minutes to familiarise ourselves with the situation and overcome any panic attacks. When we were satisfied that our masks were keeping out the gas we moved towards the exit door, told to remove masks, the door was thrown open and we staggered out into the fresh air, only it wasn't that fresh in the immediate vicinity of the chamber as some gas escaped through the open door and we took some with us on our clothing. To remove the gas sticking to us we were told to

move about and wave our arms in the air. All well and good if there was a wind blowing! Most of us had inhaled some gas as we left the chamber having removed masks and this caused us to cough and splutter but it all passed off after a few minutes. And there were no lasting effects.

That was the first experience. On later occasions we were shown how to eat and drink whilst in the chamber or if there was a gas attack. The procedure was to take in a breath through the respirator, then hold breath. Lift away the respirator from the chin thus exposing the mouth, place a small piece of bread in the mouth, replace the mask and blow out the breath. This laborious method was to be adopted for the whole piece of bread and also to take a sip of water. Nobody dare ask how to eat a steak and chips or drink a pint of Boddingtons, or if the food would be safe to eat after being exposed to the gas while eating or drinking.

That at least was the theory. Luckily we didn't have to do it for real.

Training, going away at the weekend or on Annual Camp evokes different memories, emotions and levels of enthusiasm from every individual. For an un-military mind, Captain Mary Freeman's memories could evoke horror about why anyone should join the TA, but what also comes through is a strong sense of fun, comradeship and working through adversity:

The weekend training took place at Holcombe Brook, Kimnel Park, Dale Barracks Chester, Leek (both of these prior to modernisation), Swynnerton, Proteus,

Figure 48 NBC training in the 1970s

Nesscliffe, Capel Curig, Halton, Warcop, Burtonwood, Hurst Green, Wathgill and Scarborough amongst others which I can no longer bring to mind.

At Hurst Green we billeted in the Church Hall – girls slept on the stage with the curtains drawn and the boys slept in the auditorium. At Burtonwood, we slept on the floor of disused prefabs. We were issued with brown paper to put under our groundsheets as the walls & floors were always soaking wet.

I remember doing a night exercise at Burtonwood in the depth of winter; we had to pair up and dig trenches in clay. It took ages to break through the frost which covered the clay and then it began to rain. John Williams and I had managed to dig a deep enough trench to hide in (I think we conned Geoff Ashmore into starting it off as he was a road digger by trade) so thought we were OK. Not so; the trench began to fill up with water as the clay wouldn't absorb it. We tried to keep dry by putting the ponchos at the bottom but they eventually began to float so we had to jam ourselves against the sides of the trench and, to keep warm, tucked our feet under each other's armpits. The only thing which stopped us from getting hypothermia was a fire fight. It's strange how adrenalin makes one forget everything. We were up and fighting immediately although I doubt we would have hit many targets!! It was the same night that our patrol just happened to take us under the motorway café and we just happened to pop in for a cup of tea. We thought we were behaving sensibly by placing all our weapons in a pile under the table and leaving someone on guard but we got hauled over the coals the following morning as we had apparently caused major alarm to the public.

Captain Mary Freeman RAMC

Figure 49 Geoff Ashmore

Training is essentially provided to make a citizen into a soldier. The qualities required by a soldier include: militarism, fitness and leadership. The Army's training endeavours to meet these requirements. Collective or core training is mandatory, and is aimed at fulfilling the unit's potential war role. The next level of training is aimed at individuals, and is designed to enhance their skills clinically and militarily so as to function more efficiently within a unit sub-group i.e. a ward area, or to enable them to be proficient enough to deploy within the Regular Army without extended assimilation.

Junior Officer Courses, Sergeants' Courses are all rites of passage as Corporal Tom Howell describes:

In February (1942) I was sent on a Sergeants course at Boyce Barracks in Aldershot. Four weeks of intensive work. Drill by Guard NCOs most mornings. Lectures by MOs and lectures on military administration. We had many tentage drills concentrating mainly on "Tents Hospital Expanding", until we became proficient at erecting them. The position of each piquet post and tent peg allocation and guy ropes being critical. The significance of this became apparent later.

As the individual prepares himself the unit as a whole has to regularly experience working with other units, TA or Regular, ensuring it is proficient in the role expected of it at that particular time. Tom Howell now Captain and Adjutant of 127 Field Ambulance re-lives such an exercise:

1963 saw the biggest military gathering since the war. EXERCISE SCAMPERDOWN was held on Salisbury Plain. Army Divisions from Scotland downwards were deployed for nearly a week. It revealed that lessons learned the hard way in war had been half forgotten. Many personnel were new to the Army having joined the TA post-war. Start Points/Release points for vehicle convoys were being missed, lack of discipline in timings, and many snarl-ups at night in wet weather were reminders of battles of the past

Commanding Officers realised the deficiency in role, and endeavoured to make the training as realistic as possible. They recognise that medical units do not exist independently, and require the co-operation of many other units of all arms to function. This principle was at the centre of EXERCISE GREEN OCTOPUS as Colonel Elder explains:

I'd been to the Staff College and spoken to one or two of my contemporises. We decided we could do an exercise which would involve other units i.e. the Marines, Transport, Police, Engineers and so on, and more than one medical unit. We'd have two hospitals, a Field Ambulance and so on, and then we'd evacuate with helicopters and whatever vehicles we had available through the whole chain of evacuation from the front line right through to the General Hospital, in a compressed scale so we could manage it. We had well over a thousand people taking part, and it was called Green Octopus.

It was held initially between Swynnerton and Leek and then later on we did it between Swynnerton and Nesscliffe. One time we did it between Swynnerton, Leek and Nesscliffe, it became a very big thing. It was cancelled once because Mrs Thatcher cut the petrol allowance for the TA. The funding was minimal; we had to fund it out of our own resources in terms of petrol, ammunition and training days.

The overall objective was to exercise the medical units in a hostile environment as near to a war situation as we could manage. It ran for a few years

I am glad to say being a Scots man eventually it was translated by our Admin Officer Peter Bond, who went up to Scotland as SO2 Med at Head Quarters Scotland and it became Exercise Tartan Octopus and I think lasted for ten years in a similar format.

Interviewer: *Would an exercise of that proportion been possible say five or ten years previously?*

Bill: *It would have been, but it would have required the co-operation of all the people and it required, I think, a commitment. Everybody had to have their pennyworth out of it, you know. You couldn't get the Military Police to lay out a route and all the rest of it, if they weren't going to be involved in it. It was an exercise for them as well as us, the same with the Signals. The Signals were far too elaborate to begin with and we had "gin palace"- type vehicles and a huge network of stuff which took about a day to set up. That wasn't the idea but we had to adapt a Signal Regiment which was for use to Germany in a war to our little campaign in north Derbyshire so it was all very much a learning curve for everybody.*

Figure 50 Evacuating casualties during EXERCISE GREEN OCTOPUS, year unknown

Figure 51 Colonel Elder with Lieutenant Colonel Mavis Plant (Matron) thought to have been taken at Swynnerton Camp 1976 during EXERCISE GREEN OCTOPUS

Standing alongside basic military and clinical training is adventurous and higher level arduous training, which seek to develop the individual to higher levels of military skills and fitness, arguably one of the key factors why people are attracted to the TA and are retained within the service. In 2009 Captain Alan Fortuin led an intrepid group of 207 personnel to Morocco for high level trekking, including an ascent of Mont Toukbal, the highest peak in North Africa. In earlier years competition training was the main focus for those members of the unit who wanted to do something a little different from normal training.

Figure 52 Manchester Medics on top of Mount Toubkal, Morocco, Armed Forces Day 2009

Pegasus training during the 1970s to the 90s was a medical competition open to all TA and Regular units aimed at developing higher levels of military skills.

> **Steve:** *In the Pegasus competition, we'd go out map reading, orienteering and route marching up and down roads. You'd learn about helicopter handling and marshalling. It was a competition thing but you learnt all these different military skills.*
>
> **Interviewer:** *So it was fairly physical?*
>
> **Steve:** *It was and we used to have to put in at least an extra weekend per month on top of the normal training where we were doing the*

catering. This extra weekend was where you'd go away, put your greens on, do your marching, do your walking, learn from grid references. Learn how to survive in the field, and it was a very good competition and the unit used to excel in the Pegasus competition. There weren't many times where we didn't come within the first three if not win it.

As a young group, we used to do it all the time; we used to enter all competitions. The unit used to thrive on it. The training was fantastic for new recruits because whenever they went down to Aldershot they'd come back rated as Top Recruit. We never sent anyone down unless they had been thoroughly trained in all military aspects. But from our point of view we didn't just do the chefing, myself and Mark and quite a few other young guys we'd go out and want to do the military side of it as well.

Sergeant Steve Randall RLC

Individuals join the TA for a variety of reasons and remain committed as long as the whole TA ethos remains attractive to them. Retention is a fine balance between meeting the expectations of the individual, and the demands of the service. Work, family commitments, health and personal training demands made by the TA may all combine to shorten careers. Those individuals who choose to stay in the TA for over three years invariably stay for long periods of time, benefiting from its camaraderie and the military life offered. Captain Malcolm Jackson points out that whilst the TA has a lot to offer for the committed, this abundance of choice causes its own problems.

Getting a team together is often more difficult than first anticipated:

Yes – it is difficult; we have always had a shooting team, and we used to have annual events at Altcar on

Figure 53 A young Private Steve Randall taken in 1976

the ranges where we would have a Brigade Skill At Arms Meeting, where all the local units TA and Regular would compete. That weekend was a big range weekend, and on Sunday the families could come, there would be a tent set up, there would be a band playing. It was a very pleasant weekend for everybody – but as the TA shrank, these events have been held less and less. So now we have a Medical Brigade SAAM at Strensall, but shooting is an important aspect of the Army. Unfortunately, I feel being in the Medical Corps there is a lot of emphasis to keep people on the medical side trained up, so it is always a balance, there are lots of other activities in the Army which people enjoy doing, whether it is skiing or Nijmegen Training and Pegasus in the old days. Invariably the same enthusiastic individual is involved in both Pegasus and the shooting team – it does lead to some conflict of interest sometimes.

Captain Malcolm Jackson

Figure 54 Manchester Medics winning the female Pegasus competition in 1984

Walking or marching has been, and remains, an enduring pastime in military circles.

The forced route march gave way to the 15 mile walk, historically part of the basic fitness test. More arduous marches took place noticeably the Chichester Marches.

The Nijmegen Walks in Holland continue to cater for the individual who wants to push and test themselves physically.

Annual Camps invariably go in three year cycles. One year individual training, followed by career and Adventurous training and finally a Collective training, often as a hospital exercise. Up to the 1960s, these exercises took place on Salisbury Plain before later going to the Continent. More recently, with the prospect of mobilisation the TA has taken advantage of purpose-built hospital training facilities initially at Saighton, Chester and then at Strensall, York.

Annual Camps are remembered by the individual for a variety of reasons; where they were held, the people who went, events that happened, the weather and how much or not they enjoyed it. Lieutenant Colonel Marie Farmer illustrates this point in respect of the 1972 Camp

Figure 55 Nurses of 12 CCS on Annual Camp, Woowich 1961. Marie Farmer is kneeling on the left of the centre row

Interviewer: Which camps did you use in Britain?

Marie: Barry Budden in Scotland and Garelochead. Barry Budden was on the east coast near Dundee and Garelochead was on the Glasgow side. At Garelochead, I tell you what, it was the worst weather ever. It absolutely poured with rain and we were in tents. We always went Whit week, I think because of the Manchester holidays. The week we got back it was sun shining!

This was Lieutenant Colonel Farmer's first camp as Matron.

For others, different factors are important as Major Colin Gidman articulates:

Interviewer: So what in your period, for whatever reason, do you think has been the best camp you've been to in the TA?

Colin: It's a very difficult question to decide that. We had a fantastic time at Crowbrough, a group of us spent 10 or 11 days in the field and the rest of the unit came out in small batches, and that was a fantastic camp. I've been to Gibraltar with the unit where we were treated as infanteers from day one - a fantastic camp. But I think the most comfortable camp in the sense of feeling you were part of a unit was Saighton, Camp Chester. It was taken over as a derelict camp by Brigadier Bryn Francis, who was the Brigadier in charge of Ops and Planning for the Royal Army Medical Corps, as a Field Training Centre, and we were the first unit in there in 1987. It was literally falling about our ears. We did a lot of work and we had made it a fantastic camp. It could take a Field Hospital or, as it was then, a General Hospital, comfortably. We had a proper Sergeants Mess, and an Officers' Mess and the camp could take four or five hundred people, which these days you can't, and certainly you don't get the messes or the NAAFIs. Messes are part and parcel of being in the Army; you need to know how to live and to behave in a Mess, be it a Sergeants' Mess, an Officers' Mess or even a Junior Ranks' Club!

Crowbrough 1995, as Major Gidman recalls, was the first Annual Camp attended by ex-Royal Regiment of Fusiliers soldiers, who joined the unit following Options for Change. They facilitated a comprehensive military skills package. When the training facilities were closed at

Saighton, 207 became the first unit to use the new hospital training facilities at Strensall in 1999.

Real-time medical cover, mainly at air shows, was an integral part of Annual Camps for a ten year period in the 1990s and provided many highlights. Luckily, the unit's medical skills were not seriously called into action even when two Russian MIGs collided in mid-air at RAF Fairford in 1993.

1997 saw the possibility of two Camps. The main effort was at Redford Cavalry Barracks, Edinburgh. Individuals then had the option of going to either Gibraltar or the Ascension Islands in the South Atlantic. For those who chose the latter it proved to be a unique experience on a volcanic, tropical island.

Training is anticipation and readiness for war. This present generation of soldiers foresaw the possibility of mobilisation as the Twin Towers disappeared in smoke and flames whilst at Annual Camp in 2001. Training since then has, and continues, to be predominantly based towards active service. Similar stories come down through history as soldiers sense, (as Private Tom Howell recalls in 1939) "seeing the writing on the wall". Times may change but the personal requirements to meet the challenge remain.

Figure 56 Manchester Medics in the Ascension Islands 1997

Keeping the Peace

The historical association between the TA and their local community had seen many TA centres built and maintained by the boards of Trustees. Many were listed buildings of historical value. The amalgamation and disbandment of infantry battalions meant that that local barracks and potential new soldiers became available.

The Royal Regiment of Fusiliers was to lose its presence at Ashton-Under-Lyne and the serving soldiers were given the option to re-badge as medics. A significant number took up this option. The then Captain Gidman outlines the medical perspective in selling the "medics" to hardened Fusiliers.

Interviewer: Can you remember coming here and being greeted by a load of Fusiliers

Colin: I came here in August 1993, with some very hostile looking Infanteers looking at me on the first night. So, being a good, polite medic, I put my RSM's hat on and introduced myself. I'd brought with me a Captain Karen Berry, who was the wife of Captain Tony Berry, another ex-regular RSM who had come back into the unit. And we set about talking to different groups of what the way forward was. They were now transferring cap badges from Infanteers, which was a bit of a shock to some of them, to becoming medics.

Interviewer: What was the process of changing a cap badge from a Fusilier to a medic?

Colin: Well, it was voluntary, if they wanted to be in the TA, the nearest TA Infantry was in Ardwick.

Interviewer: What was expected of them to change?

Colin: Within three years they had to qualify to Combat Medical Technician Class 1 to maintain their current rank. For example they were given the opportunity to stay a Sergeant as long as they qualified within three years.

We took over about 50 Fusiliers. For the first two weeks, we did medical training with them and we brought in Staff Sergeant Mary Ward and WO2 Charles Rowland. Some decided they had to leave, it wasn't for them. Some of the wives of the infanteers found out we had females here, and it definitely wasn't for them – they weren't going to let their husbands go away on weekends with strange females. So we levelled out at about 30 to 35 people and of those we've still got some remaining now who have gone from the rank of private Infanteers to being private medics and are now Sergeants in the Unit and some have reached the rank of WO2.

The Fusiliers had their own reservations about the proposed changes as Corporal Martin Clarey recalls:

Interviewer: *So, when things were changing with the Fusiliers, how did they break the news to you about who was going to take over here at Ashton?*

Martin: *It came through the rumour lines as usual, and then one Tuesday on parade, they walked in and said: "Oh next year you are not Fusiliers any more, you are going to be medics".*

There was a big groan and "Oh God, no, no!" and "I'm leaving", but out of the unit fifteen of us stayed and carried on and did the study and worked our way up.

Interviewer: *So how did they sell it you at that time, did somebody from 207 come up here and sell it to you?*

Martin: *We had various visits and little snippets of what we were doing, 207 at that time was a General Hospital not a Field Hospital and I think that's what put a lot of the old Fusiliers against coming over, because they'd be going to a Corps instead of infantry and the close-knitness of being out there in the field. They tried to sell it to us, saying that: "No, you'll have a close-knit community in the Hospital and it's a different way of living". I went to Gibraltar as a Fusilier and we had two SNCOs, one of whom was Staff Carter who had just left 207. He came out there, told us what 'idiots' medics are and how much they like the beer the same as us and I think that's what swayed the fifteen of us to stay. I think a few more were going to stay but age was against them. The actual mental training as a medic was a bit against them as they all said - they're 'grunts' as Fusiliers, and I think they were worried about changing from being out in the field to having someone's life in your hands was a big change for them. Some of them did move out but they stayed in the TA and moved to other infantry units and did very well for themselves. The ones who stayed with the medics are all working their way up.*

In 1997, 207 took over the famous Castle Armoury at Bury, establishing a new squadron. 207 had returned in terms of squadron numbers to pre-Option for Change levels.

Reserve Forces Act 1996

The use of the reservist reservoir "going back to the colours" historically underpins the logistical planning for a large-scale war. The "call out of the TA" had always been considered likely in similar circumstances providing a pool of experienced, if not recently trained soldiers.

Figure 57 Sergeant Martin Clarey on Annual Camp at Penhale in 2011

The TA has always had restrictions placed upon their usage. Prior to the Great War the TA were not allowed to mobilise for overseas service, though many waived this right. This restriction was re-instated after the War in 1921 due to a perceived lack of regard by the War Office that was felt by many TA members who saw their peers, stranded in India and not de-mobilised until 1919-20. Similar problems were encountered prior to WW2 but were quickly addressed ensuring the TA and their estates became pivotal in the mobilisation process. More recently, prior to the First Gulf War 1991, with little legislative support, particularly in employment rights, TA members who wished to deploy had to negotiate time off with their employer, many came back to no job at all.

The use of TA medical staff during the First Gulf War had centred upon the mobilisation of a single unit with individuals from throughout the Army Medical Services augmenting and bringing the hospital establishment up to strength. The administrative processes to allow this, as Carver [40] outlines, were considerable and resulted in a radical re-assessment of how best to use the TA. The Volunteers were to become a significant minority of the future armed services but would provide a sizeable majority of the highly specialised and professional individuals and groups such as the medical services, required for any conflict. Significant in this respect was the Reserve Forces Act 1996, which secured the employment rights of any individual called up for service. The Act enshrined in law the Government's obligation to those individuals who were to be compulsorily mobilised. Earnings, pension rights and employment status, were to be guaranteed. The umbrella of the Act made possible a more robust use of the TA. The Balkans became the first theatre to significantly use the TA. They were not deployed collectively but individually, as an augment. The process being coordinated through Reserves Training and Mobilisation Centre (RTMC) near Chilwell, Nottingham.

Individual deployment was the norm. The TA individuals were called on when needed on a purely voluntary basis (Intelligent Mobilisation) and this was coordinated through the RTMC.

The Balkans

In 1992, British troops were sent to the Balkans as part of a United Nations Protection Force, initially to Croatia and then to Bosnia. Ethnic cleansing became the murderous consequence of Europe's first internal conflict since WW2. Peace keeping as opposed to war making became the accepted role of the Army in this era. As the political process of constructing new states progressed, the continual demands on a reduced Army were significant. By 1997, there were 4,822 British troops in Bosnia of whom 989 were Territorials, 207 personnel were either attached to Divisional or Brigade Headquarters or to Regular

Figure 58 Ilydsa Hospital, Sarajevo. The marks in the wall have been caused by small arms fire (2000)

Army Units in a medical capacity. The TA medics were in demand, and 207 saw many individuals go to serve, the majority going via the newly opened RTMC Chilwell. President Milosevic of Serbia continued to spread his ethnic and nationalistic ambitions until his downfall and arrest in 2000. British Troops were at the forefront of the humanitarian and peace keeping forces, and 207 personnel deployed to Macedonia and Kosovo.

Notable in this deployment was Corporal Jo Tamblyn (from Macclesfield Detachment) who was attached to General Rose's HQ staff and was awarded the Queen's Commendation for Valuable Service. In a letter to the Unit she describes the conditions she found herself in;

Finally I've got a few minutes to put pen to paper.

Just a quick note to say hello and let you know I'm alive and well and actually quite enjoying myself, despite everything.

We were messed around at Catterick really. Didn't properly sort out money etc. I was on the first coach out of Catterick at midnight on Saturday 17th December. Should have been catching flight from Brize early Sunday morning, but due to slight technical problem, found myself still sitting on the coach on a motorway service station somewhere near Nottingham, I think! Anyway, ended up in Rheindalen a few days later and a couple of days later in Italy! Me of all people got on a Herc in Bruggen and ended up night-stopping in Italy. The weather was too bad at Sarajevo and Split wouldn't take diversions!

I finally arrived in theatre on 21st December, spent first night in Zetra Stadium, sleeping in a bowling alley, - some lanes are still working! Then moved into Dalmatia Hotel in Kiseijak where I spent Christmas and New Year. Not much of a hotel by Monarch's [46] standards, but I can assure you a palace to where I am now, which is the Ilidza Complex, Hotel Terme, Sarajevo.

This place was right on the front line! I'm quite lucky, my room has a loo and it works! There are no windows just plastic sheeting and I just got a bed yesterday. Our sink doesn't work, but we have a tiny shower that you can stretch over to the sink – no hot water

---

46 Jo's civilian job was that of Air Stewardess for Monarch Airways

however. Still, I'm managing OK. I wash my hair every morning so I must be OK!

The job I'm doing is very interesting. I'm the clerk for the Joint Military Commission (JMC). Basically, I book in all the mail. Send out any post. Circulate morning mail, run around photocopying, answering telephones. Look after our lot – three Majors (One Brigadier General some of the time), and anyone else who happens to need help!

I attend the meetings with the factions and Commander so I get to see and hear history in the making. Obviously I'm involved in preparing correspondence with the parties. It's all high powered and fascinating stuff.

More in next letter. Just bumped into Les Gandy[47]

The TA soldiers, now in significant numbers, were making a valuable contribution. Their training and professionalism was noted though not always recognised as Sergeant Vinnie Marsh explains:

I went to Bosnia in 1996, my first tour. It was Op Resolute; it had just changed from Op Grapple to Op Resolute. We got called Ambulance Support Group at that time. Basically our jobs were to take any casualties in our sector to Split, which was the HQ, or get them down to the airport Divulje Barracks. We do four week stints in different locations, so we'd start four weeks in Split, four weeks in Tomislavgrad, four weeks in Sipovo, and four weeks in Gornji Vakuf. You moved around. One lad was an engineer, and obviously we were there for 6 months you'd end up going back to somewhere that you'd been before and that was the same for me when I went back to Tomislavgrad Now it was only a few weeks before we were actually leaving, we'd come to the end of our tour and I was talking to this engineer and he was saying that TA are this TA are that, they're no use, they're not like us Vinny they are not like us, you know us regular. I looked at him and said "I'm not a regular soldier mate". I said "I am now obviously because when you go on tour you sign a contract for full time service." And he like "What, what", and I said "I'm Territorial Army" and he couldn't believe it, he could not believe it. I look at that

---

47 Les Gandy was another member of 207 serving as a medic in the Balkans

as a compliment obviously, and it's not been the first time people thought I was Regular Army.....

....a lot of people have seen how involved the TA are and how much they really do want to make a contribution, and a good contribution at that. Unfortunately (and it is the same with the Regular Army) there are some who do let the side down. But hopefully now that TA units are doing far more tours – operational tours that is, hopefully the professionalism will shine through.

Soldiers from 207 were exposed to new and often dangerous environments, having to adapt their medical skills and training to their particular circumstances. The unit began to benefit from a significant number of seasoned veterans in their ranks not seen since the immediate post war era. Their operational experience was to be of considerable benefit as 207 prepared for mobilisation to Iraq in 2004.

Figure 59 Sergeant Vinny March (far right) with other members of 207, from left to right, Private Darren Smith, Lance Corporals Patrick 'Pat' Farrell and David Owen taken on their return journey from OP RESOLUTE in 1997

Second Gulf War and the Occupation of Iraq 2003-2009 (OP TELIC)

207 were at Annual Camp in 2001, at Cameron Barracks, Inverness when the events of 11 September unfolded on television. The main activity on the training programme that afternoon was PT, which took the form of volley ball.

We were out playing sport when somebody, I'm not sure who, came out and told us that a plane had gone into the World Trade Centre. We didn't believe them, so we all rushed off to the Mess and got there just as the second plane hit. We sat in silence with the odd expletive.

Captain Helen Ball

Since the First Gulf War in 1991, the possibility of a further conflict in the Middle East was prepared for. In October 2001, less than a month after the tragic events of 11September 2001, the date now universally known as 9/11, members of 207 were flying to the desert of Oman to take part in the largest British military exercise for nearly twenty years: Exercise Saif Sareea.

Figure 60 Captain Helen Ball, Helen mobilised for OP TELIC during the initial war in 2003 and returned the following year when she deployed with 207. This picture was taken on OP TELIC 4

The main aim of the exercise was to practice the deployment of an armoured brigade plus all tactical support, advancing to engage the enemy in a mobile scenario carried out in the vast expanse of arid Omani dessert. Medical support was to be led by 34 Field Hospital, who had established what was to become the prototype British Army's 50-bedded Field Hospital complex. For the medical services this large exercise was the first time that significant numbers of personnel from all the TA hospitals had been used in their operational roles as all the casualties were 'no duff'[48]. The TA went out in three tranches, all mimicking full mobilisation processes, bar the issuing of arms. The logistical implications of mobilising the TA were under scrutiny, as was the capability of the TA to respond, work effectively and be seen to cope in difficult environments. The members of 207 who went on Exercise Saif Sareea were not aware but they were at the beginning of a sequence of events which would ultimately see large numbers of TA mobilised to serve in Iraq and Afghanistan.

TA field hospitals went on a cycle of readiness to deploy for mobilisation. In 2002 under the command of Colonel Cliff Godby, 207 went up to 'R5' which signified that the unit was at a state of readiness for deployment within 30 days. One of the consequences of this advanced state of readiness was the attachment of a core of Regular Army personnel. These included Lieutenant Colonel Mike Godkin as Second in Command, Captain Stuart Horton as Adjutant (succeeded by Captain Tony Holland), Major Martin Magee Quarter Master, Major Paula Tristham as Regular Nursing Officer, Major David Cook, Training Major and Operations Officer, Warrant Officer Class One (WO1) Pat Hoyte as Regimental Sergeant Major, Warrant Officer Class Two (WO2) Stuart Harvey Regimental Quarter Master Sergeant (RQMS), Staff Sergeant Sean Carter and Sergeant Nigel Hogg all were to become integral players in the lead up to and during deployment.

2002 proved a year of growing expectation that military intervention would ensue. Afghanistan was the main focus of military activity with a mainly Regular Army commitment. Elsewhere unrelenting pressure in diplomatic circles was demanding assurances from Iraq over the status of its weapons of mass destruction, these did not appear to be forthcoming.

207 was tasked to provide medical cover for the Royal International Air Tattoo at RAF Fairford. In keeping with previous visits to the Air Tattoo an aircraft (Italian AF G22) managed to crash land on the first day, which tested the unit's response to such an episode.

---

48 'no duff' was a term used by the British Army to describe a real casualty during exercises.

In early 2003, it became apparent to most TA personnel that compulsory mobilisation would be used if the country was to go to war. The unsuccessful diplomatic exchanges with Iraq led to the creation of a coalition forces led by the USA and UK and OP TELIC (the Second Gulf War) was initiated in March 2003. The leading regular field hospitals were to be augmented by TA personnel and a TA field hospital, 202 (Midlands) was to be deployed.

I reported to the Reserves Training and Mobilisation Centre at Chilwell on Wednesday 6th March 2003. After passing the medical and dental exams, I went to get my extra clothing and kit, which consisted of one set of Combat Soldier 95 with field jacket (in green DPM) and my body armour but no rifle.

The following evening we moved to Beckingham training camp for pre-deployment training and the following Tuesday moved to the Army Medical Services Training Centre (AMSTC) at Strensall for some more training.

On the Thursday we moved to Brize Norton and after an overnight flight landed at Kuwait City Airport, where I was amazed at the heat, it was like putting your head inside an oven, and this was early March.

We moved into our acclimatisation area for a few days, and my memories are of having American Meals Ready to Eat (MREs) for lunch – including an arctic meal one day; Interesting as we had no access to any hot water to reconstitute them! Evening meal was usually of the "all in stew" type.

After a few days we took over the hospital from our regular colleagues from 33 Field Hospital, who needless to say were not too happy. This caused lots of graffiti to appear in the Portaloos.

For a tented hospital built pretty quickly in the desert, although near the Main Supply Route (MSR), it wasn't half bad, with all the usual facilities you would expect at a hospital.

The operating theatres were well equipped, and we had plenty of power supplied by the generators.

The first few days of the fighting phase saw us well versed in getting into our NBC suits and respirators, usually at night, although we did spend a few hours in them during one memorably hot day.

We had a variety of casualties, but I remember there were a high percentage of burns casualties as well as gunshot wounds and fragmentation injuries.

The facilities were beyond my expectations in so much as we had a shower block with hot running water, internet access and a large screen TV in the Mess tent which was permanently tuned into a 24 hour news channel. The food was a mixture of fresh and compo and overall was very good.

In mid-May after taking down and packing away the hospital in its entirety into ISO containers we moved up to Shaibah and took over the hospital there from 34 Field Hospital.

The facilities at Shaibah were not as good as we had been used to in Kuwait and the area also seemed more prone to sandstorms or "twisters", as they were called. These twisters had done a lot of damage to parts of the hospital and some of the accommodation prior to my arrival. Sanitation was by means of "desert roses" and "thunder boxes". The area also appeared to have more than its fair share of flies, who were always around but appeared to multiply around the cookhouse at meal times, with the result a lot of people suffered from stomach upsets. A few days after we took over, the desert roses and the thunder boxes where replaced with Portaloos which appeared to alleviate the fly problem slightly; As a result the incidence of stomach upsets decreased and people were heard to say that they were "farting with confidence".

I remember that in our tent we had a little ritual in that we would go to the Mobile Bath and Laundry Unit (MBLU) at 22:00 hours in flip flops and shorts, you didn't really need to dry yourself after, because by the time you had walked back to your tent you would be totally dry. It was still very hot, even at that time of the night.

I returned to the UK in mid-June and was de-mobbed, but on returning to TA training was warned off that 207 would be mobilising in March 2004 on OP TELIC 4.

Going back to Shaibah in late April 2004, I was amazed at the many changes that had taken place.

The hospital was still under canvas, but all the accommodation was in air conditioned Corrimecs, good ablution facilities, the *cookhouse was superb and the chefs did a fantastic job producing really fine food. We also had a gym, a library and large screen TVs.*

The EFI was open all day for tea and coffee etc. and served the "2 can" alcohol rule in the evenings. We also had an EFI shop within the accommodation lines. There was internet access and 20 minutes free phone calls a week.

A short walk away was the ECOS centre with more internet access, a large NAAFI shop, a Dutch cafeteria, Pizza Hut, BFBS and the BFPO. Just before we left a Subway franchise arrived.

How very different from Op Telic.

WO2 Jonathan 'Jon' Bell

The mobilisation process had moved on considerably since the First Gulf War. Employment rights and compensation for any loss of salary were enshrined in law. The emotional pull of family was as difficult for any generation putting themselves up for service. An informal system of volunteer gave way to compulsory mobilisation. Over sixty 207 soldiers and officers were mobilised for what became OP TELIC. As in previous deployments, 207 staff were scattered amongst the medical facilities preparing for the conflict. The majority stayed within a field hospital setting, either 34 Field Hospital or 202 Field Hospital. The enduring nature of such a conflict and the resolve to see a positive change in Iraq meant that re-enforcements were designated quickly and many other 207 personnel were mobilised to join the on-going operation.

Figure 61 Brotherly love on OP TELIC – SSgt Dave Morgan, RE, in DPM temperate (green), who served with 202 (Midlands) Field Hospital and Sgt Phil Morgan, RE, in DPM desert, who served with 16 Close Support Medical Regiment

The on-going nature of operations not just in Iraq but also concurrently in Afghanistan stretched the commitments of the Regular Army. Although individual soldiers and clinicians were deploying, this ad-hoc process placed a considerable administrative burden on the mobilising unit. Post deployment problems for the TA and Reservist, mainly with pay and health issues, were often hampered by this system failing or complicating the problem. RTMC Chilwell alleviated some of the problems by having a dedicated centre for reservists and TA; however collective mobilisation rather than individual had certain benefits, primarily in that the unit to be mobilised, if given sufficient time, could seek to address many of the protracted issues which were failing the individual.

Regular Field Hospitals were stretched and were requiring considerable augmenting from the TA. They were also experiencing deployment burn-out having being continually on operations for several years. Historically, going back as far as the Boer War it was noted that the TA will more readily mobilise as a complete unit, going with friends and colleagues rather than individuals. Addressing these problems, complete TA field hospitals with their command element were identified for mobilisation, on a rolling basis, with 207 having the honour to be the first on OP TELIC 4.

Figure 62 OP VERTITY 2003, sitting on the right is Captain Mary Freeman keeping the senior nursing staff up to date with progress

Notice was given, and the unit underwent a significant period of training culminating in the summer of 2003 in OP VERITY a validation Exercise, at 2 Medical Brigade Headquarters, Strensall, York.

On 27 March 2004, 207 (Manchester) Field Hospital (Volunteers) was mobilised on OP TELIC 4 (The UK's contribution to OPERATION IRAQI FREEDOM), to form the UK Medical Group HQ and Multi National Division (South East) (MND (SE)) Field Hospital at Shaibah Logistics Base (SLB), in Southern Iraq. SLB was a very large logistics base in the middle of the dessert 10 km south of Basra City. It also served as a transit camp for between 3–5,000 multi-national troops.

Although 207 formed the bulk of the personnel to be mobilised, plus the administrative core, the deployment was as MND (SE) Field Hospital. Numerous individuals and formed units were assigned to make up the Medical Group. Significant in this was 2 Close Support Medical Regiment (CSMR) a regular unit based in Germany, who would provide the ambulance services and staff many of the outlying medical facilities. The logistical element to the Medical Group was provided by 152 (Ulster) Transport Regiment RLC(V).

Figure 63 Hospital on Parade, final preparations in York before departing for OPTAG at Lydd. The squad to the left of the picture are the logistical section made up mainly of 152 (Ulster) Transport Regiment

Assigned medical personnel came from all the other TA field hospitals. A significant number were Regular Army personnel, particularly doctors. The Royal Navy provided four MA (Medical Assistants) and AELOs (Air Evacuation Liaison Officer) came from the RAF.

On the 27 March 2004, all 207 staff to be deployed paraded at the Armoury in Stockport, and following a hearty goodbye, were driven by coach to RTMC Chilwell in Nottingham. The unit stayed overnight here, collecting kit and completing medical examinations. An unfortunate few were not fit enough to go and left to return home disappointed. On 28 March, the unit moved to Strensall to undertake pre-deployment training. This was the first time that that all personnel had come together. Integration through training followed with an all-inclusive group identity forming. The formation took up its deployment title, MND (SE) Field Hospital. To our surprise after three weeks training, the Unit was stood down for the Easter weekend. The true reality of operational service became more apparent as soldiers said farewell again to their loved ones on the certainty of going overseas. Operational Training and Advisory Group (OPTAG) training took place at Lydd in Kent. This training, specific to Operations included mine clearance, basic language skills in Arabic, the use of translators

Figure 64 Winding down after a day's training at Lydd. The Second in Command, Lieutenant Colonel Mike Godkin (with ball) next to, him with his back to the camera, is the then Corporal Martin Clarey

Figure 65 Captain Sharon Wright checking and sending last minute messages before flying out of Brize Norton

and a theatre update. With all training complete the hospital staff made the long journey back to York. On 28 April the Unit finally embarked at Brize Norton, initially to Qatar by RAF Tri-Star and then onto Basra in a C130 Hercules. Not all staff flew at the same time, and all personnel were finally together on 1 May 2004. The hospital personnel were initially accommodated in a tented transit camp for acclimatisation. The weather was un-seasonal and staff had to endure rain in the desert and a series of sandstorms, including one that ripped through the female tent.

207 were to take over from 22 Field Hospital. During this transitional stage, the newly arrived staff were quickly called into action as an American convoy, transiting through our Area of Responsibility (AOR), was attacked with sufficient casualties to have a major incident declared. The new staff performed to such a high professional standard that no validation exercise was required for take over and 207 officially took control of the MND (SE) Hospital on 3 May 2004.

The Hospital was housed under canvas. Seventy five ward beds were available, with the capability to expand up to 200. The Hospital was designed with a central corridor or spine 150 meters long, onto which all wards and departments joined. Casualties mainly arrived by helicopter, with the landing site situated 50 meters in front of the Accident and Emergency (A&E) Department. The more intensive departments were situated at the front of the hospital with the wards and physiotherapy departments to the rear. Corimecs, metal boxes not dissimilar to ISO containers, were the versatile building blocks which provided the accommodation blocks and all the major facilities within the base. Showers and toilet facilities for the hospital were in corimecs situated mainly outside the wards. The Command Post, armoury and Motor Transport (MT) section were based in the main accommodation area, 200 meters from the hospital. A large cookhouse provided a daily focus along with a NAAFI store and café/bar.

The hospital was a small element of a huge base, which was shared with the other units comprising the UK Battle Group. A contingent of Dutch infantry was also on the base with their medical support. Troops entering or leaving Iraq would invariably transit through SLB, and in the summer of 2004 the base was very busy.

Figure 66 Sun rise over MND (SE) Field Hospital, A&E

Figure 67 Sun rise over MND (SE) Field Hospital, wards

Deployed medical staff are expected to go where their skills are required. Several 207 personnel found themselves working not in the main hospital, but in outlying posts within the AOR or with elements of CSMR based in SLB as part of the ambulance crew. Examples of this would be Captain Rob Rouse, an A&E nurse who was to be utilised in several hotspot areas from Al Amarah to Umm Qasr, dental nurse Lance Corporal Lucy Stoddart spent her tour at Basra Palace and CMT Corporal Yvonne Flanagan who was a crew commander on the Blue light Matrix. Medical personnel from SLB were expected to perform clinics in the various military bases within the AOR. Specialist medical services did regular clinics in the outlying posts exposing themselves to significant risk in trying to care for their patients as Major Alan Taberner, Officer Commanding (OC) of the Field Mental Health Team (FMHT) describes;

I visited the Battle Group (BG) in Camp Abu Najif, in Al Amarah flying by Chinook helicopter, an 80 minute ride. It flew tactically, weaving about the sky to dodge potential Surface to Air Missiles (SAM) or small arms fire on nearing the base. The previous week it was shot at, but this time it was uneventful – phew, it was good to stand on 'terra firma' and be in control again. Camp Abu Najif is an isolated British fortress camp north of Basra city, said to be in 'bandit' country and regularly subjected to mortaring. The FMHT was kept busy with the BG's trauma stress experiences, mental health education, advice and working with commanders. When I returned to SLB I discovered that one of our [ground] escorts had been ambushed in Basra city and a shootout took place. The insurgents eventually withdrew and there were no British casualties. I reflected on the fact that I usually travelled on that run but had visited Al Amarah instead.

That ambush had involved the hospital's OC physiotherapist, Captain Sharon Wright.

Events locally are never as seen on television. The edited portrayal for home viewers tells a story which the public can only be partially aware, as the news only allows five minutes to get a story across which is continually evolving, and as ever open to political interpretation. Troops on the ground have to be involved and made aware of current and planned operations. MND (SE) Hospital held daily Orders Groups (O Groups) headed by OC Hospital Squadron Lieutenant Colonel Kerry Trow. In what became a daily ritual, the Hospital Squadron Sergeant Major, WO2 Richard 'Ricky' Stock, disseminated the daily news in a format all troops could understand:

Figure 68 Major Alan Taberner showing his softer side – or is it lunch!!

141

H.M.C
Nightly Brief

Please read the following note from today's (Date 05/05/04) brief, J2

1. Al-Amarah is still not the place to be! Mortars are being fired on a regular basis & small arms fire now meets every helicopter on its arrival, as two Pumas found out to their dismay! RPGs have also been fired at helicopters, but no reports of casualties. A Police Station in an up-market area of Basra was also subject to a mortar attack. A new tactic is for the bombers to mark the sites of IEDs with bricks or sandbags hanging off wires etc. This acts as a warning to the locals, as to what is about to happen. Worrying, but more so when at one such site the local Police moved away from the site!!
2. Again, no tomorrow's weather report, though I did ask. 2nd GD to Lt. Col. Trow.
3. Be alert to thefts, they're on the increase in SLB, but the RMP are increasing their presence.
4. Dress policy reared its ugly head again. In the hospital, unless for clinical reasons, you WILL wear combat trousers & T-shirt as a minimum. Shorts are a no-no, so advise your friends coz I know you all comply. Outside the complex, wear uniform & hat unless engaged in vigorous work.
5. Oh yes, Al-Amarah is still out of bounds to vehicles & tomorrow's flight in has been cancelled.
6. So, it's still a dangerous World out there.

CO's points

1. As above regarding dress policy.
2. Don't befriend the LEC's!! One of them has just been fired for 'getting involved' with a female member of the forces, no further info supplied!

RPG – Rocket Propelled Grenade
LEC - Locally Employed Civilian
GD - General Duties

Figure 69 WO2 Ricky Stock RAMC

Iraq in 2004 was still a country in transition. All the major civilian institutions from the police, army and significantly the Iraqi health service were in a process of re-establishing themselves after the war and the rule of the Ba'athist Saddam era. 207 as MND (SE) Hospital had invariably to care for many local Iraqis, some injured fighting as insurgents. These proved difficult to nurse as they were often on the same ward as the British troops they had been firing on. Civilians were brought to the front gate of SLB. A&E staff were delegated to assess the patients to ensure that only life, limb or sight threatening injuries were admitted to the hospital. Many chronic conditions presented but the hospital had no onward process to discharge individuals to the community as in the UK. The local hospital in Basra had many shortfalls one being no burns unit. The Hospital was asked to deal with burns patients many of them children. The Army contacted the Chain of Hope charity for help for a number of seriously ill children. Two Iraqi children, with their fathers as escort, were successfully flown to the UK for essential cardiac surgery. The wards staff at SLB, Lieutenant Colonel Allagoa and her colleagues did the medical assessments and the Hospital Management Cell (HMC) staff dealt with the significant bureaucratic problems. The treatment of children presented significant problems as then there was no paediatric equipment readily available;

similarly no paediatricians or children's nurses are employed by the forces. 207 had to rely on staff who had extensive children's experience and were working in civilian roles such as Health Visitors.

During May 2004 the military situation in Al Amarah deteriorated and the outpost there found itself under daily fire by small arms or mortar by a large number of militia insurgents laying siege. British operations to regain control of the area led to many injuries and unfortunately several deaths. The local British Battle Group – Princess of Wales's Royal Regiment was said to be the most attacked unit in the whole of the Iraqi theatre of operations. A soldier from this regiment Private Johnson Beharry was seriously injured on 11 June 2004, he was stabilised at the hospital and subsequently evacuated by air (Aeromed) to Kuwait. For his actions in Al Amarah he was awarded the Victoria Cross.

On 23 June 2004, the Commanding Officer, Colonel Godby, handed over command of UK Medical Group to the incoming Commanding Officer of 207 Colonel Bhatnagar, and left the Field Hospital in style on a camel, with troops lining the road to the gate; a leaving event to remember.

Figure 70 WO2 Jon Bell carrying one of our young casualties back to ITU after surgery

Figure 71 On the right is Colonel Godby (the outgoing CO), on the left Colonel Bhatnagaer (the incoming CO)

The main group of casualties coming through the hospital were, as in any conflict, the result of the environment. Heat injuries, diarrhoea and vomiting were constant bed fillers. The desert heat began to take its toll as Major Alan Taberner explains

> *The constant searing heat averaged 47°C, that wasn't much less indoors, sapped energy. These temperatures steadily rose to a maximum of 64.6°C in July playing on my mind because the environment was so dry and bland, I wished to see green grass, rain and smell the English countryside. This was instead of body sweat, and local petro-chemical refinery plants and our generators polluting the air with lingering oil smells. The heat was like sticking your head in an oven and breathing in – hot air on the breath, which became unbearable if you stayed in it too long.*

The Hospital was operating in desert conditions. For the Hospital to function utilities such as water, electricity and communications had to be constantly operational. Unfortunately, all were prone to stop when needed most. The Hospital had four large generators for electricity, but they were totally unreliable in the heat of the desert and kept tripping out. In one incident, the lights failed when a patient was on the operating table and the surgeons had to continue using head lights. Water had to be brought in by tankers by road. Any disruption in this process would invariably result in shortages felt keenly by the staff;

> *Water was rationed to one shower a day and only to run water to rinse soap off. Laundry was often suspended so clothes were dried and re-worn. During water rationing, toilets were sealed off, having to use portaloos which really hummed in the heat! Drinking water was bottled and there's no shortage of that, however after only 10 – 15 minutes out of the fridge it became hot water.*

> *Major Alan Taberner QARANC*

The HMC had to manage the Hospital with a constant expectation that one or all the utility services would be non-operational. The air conditioning was a constant concern, not just for the patients but also for some of the electronic equipment used within the HMC with some computers, when not in use, being stored in the department fridge. Staff working in other areas, such as the pathology department, with sensitive equipment would have to rely on helping hands to move blood stocks to a designated cool van.

As the tour progressed staff were allowed 36 hours leave in nearby Kuwait to enjoy the sea and proper sand. The political situation was continually evolving in Iraq. Geoff Hoon the Minister for Defence visited the SLB and the Hospital on 14 June in the run up to handing over power to an interim Iraqi Government at the beginning of July. In an attempt to minimise any violent action on the day the handover was brought forward to 28 June. Unfortunately it was marked as one of the blackest days, as violence in Basra erupted with the death of a young soldier. The Daily Mirror's publication of hoax pictures of British abuse of Iraqis and real images of actual abuse of internees at the United States of America facility in Abu Ghraib added further to the uncertainty of the troops on the ground and having to deal with the backlash. The capture of a Royal Marine craft with its crew by Iran again heightened tension. Fortunately they were all released without harm and were evacuated back through the hospital at SLB.

Dark moments where interjected with funny moments such as when an American Black Hawk helicopter flew in, and tried to land on the Red Cross next to the Field Hospital. The down draft nearly blew the hospital down. Skilfully, a quick witted soldier moved forward to vector it away to the recognised landing site. Apparently the Americans use a cross to mark their landing site; we British use the letter 'H'. (Our Red Cross indicates to aircraft that it is a medical facility). Another stress reliever was the "Combat Salsa" dance lessons taken by Major Taberner. Whilst in Iraq the Euro 2004 Football competition was taking place due to the time difference those keen enough had to stay up until 2am to watch the live matches.

207 staff had now found their feet on operations, none more so than probably the oldest soldier in Iraq, Captain Malcolm Jackson who at 62 years of age was OC Pathology, and revelled in the experience:

Interviewer: How did you find your deployment?

Malcolm: I quite enjoyed myself in Iraq in many ways. After spending twenty years pretending to do something, to actually do the real thing was great. I had a proper equipped laboratory with two staff. We ran it very similarly to NHS guidelines, with clinical governance, health and safety, meetings and what have you. It was multi-disciplinary, so I would do microbiology in the morning and switch to haematology in the afternoon. There were three of us; and we worked it so that the person who had been on nights, would

Figure 72 Captain Malcolm Jackson

Figure 73 Major Sharon "Queen of the Mops" Stewart

Figure 74 Major Val Johnson (front row, sitting wearing dark brown t-shirts) with members of her theatre staff, both UK and Czech

take the following afternoon off if it was quiet, and two of us would run the lab.....

.....X-ray, who were with us found it very difficult as they were just two, they were doing every second night on call.

Other staff were becoming associated with their role. Major Sharon Stewart and her staff on Ward 3 became known as the "mop queens" because of their on-going attempt to rid the isolation ward of sand and dust. Attached staff had integrated very well. A&E under the command of Major William Jamieson proved a very efficient area capable of responding to anything that came their way. In early July MND SE Staff were augmented by a Czech Surgical Team. Major Val Johnson, OC theatres quickly embracing them into the British way of doing things.

With the transition of power certain outposts were given back to the Government, noticeably Basra Palace, the former Saddam complex which had been used as 1 Mechanised Brigade's BG HQ, situated on the banks of the Shaat Al Arab. Medical provision moved to the Shaat Al Arab Hotel north of Basra City. Commander Medical was based in the expanding military facilities at Basra Airport. Medical facilities were also expanding due to the increasing number of soldiers at this location which resulted in some hospital staff being transferred to the airport.

The insurgent threat continued to rise. The Madhi Army was becoming a significant protagonist in Basra, which had become a more volatile area with increasing sectarian violence within the Iraqi community. It came as little surprise that on 4 August 2004 SLB came under attack for the first time. The mortars exploded without causing any harm. All staff were expected to wear helmets and body armour whilst walking between facilities, and have them close by if working. The first week in August there was considerable unrest in Basra. Warriors Armoured Personal Carriers and Challenger 2 Tanks could be seen speedily exiting the base towards another incident. Unfortunately this invariably resulted in more casualties, which was not the induction our relief, 256 Field Hospital (Volunteers) wanted.

The Command elements of 256 arrived on 4 August the main body arriving to commence their handover from 7 August. As more of their staff arrived 207 personnel were gradually stood down to begin their packing. The unit flew home in two tranches, the majority of the staff on the first tranche on 11 August and the second, with the command element, on the 15 August.

We flew home on the 15 August 2004 initially in a C-130 Hercules to Qatar and I remember that the G force was tremendous when it rose suddenly and banked around to avoid missiles. My feet were solid on the floor and I couldn't move them, and then all of a sudden they started to float out of control – a really amazing but nauseous experience. I thought I might have vomited but deep breathing held it off. The rest of the one hour ride was boring, noisy and uncomfortable. At Qatar we changed to an RAF Tri-Star for the return journey to the UK. We were processed through the Reserves Training and Mobilisation Centre at Chilwell and the first thing that I noticed was dampness, colour (especially greenery) and the fresh smells of England. It was good to be back.

Major Alan Taberner QARANC

The Unit performed very well during its first period of mobilisation. Attached staff where embraced and made to feel part of the Unit. The difficult and at times dangerous environment brought out the best in people. Flexibility of working and a desire to get the best possible result for all in their care exemplified the ethos of all staff.

Up until the end of the OP TELIC campaign in 2009 the Unit continued to provide personnel who mobilised as individuals. But in 2006 the then CO, Colonel Bhatnagar, became the first member of 207 to deploy to Afghanistan as the Consultant Physician to the Bastion Hospital.

Bastion to Bury

Apart from bikers, we don't get a lot of trauma injuries in England anymore, particularly since seat belt legislation. What I will see and learn in Afghanistan in six weeks I would not see in six years in the NHS ... I don't really see it as my job to comment on whether we should or should not be at war –I just think that if there are people out there with injuries and I have the skills to help, then it is my job to go. My parents were shocked at first when I told them about my deployment to Afghanistan, but they support me in anything that I want to do. They think it is a great opportunity for me and they are proud of me.

Captain Jill Rutherford – Davies (extracted from the RAMC magazine June 2010)

207 Field Hospital's preparation for deployment to Afghanistan is set in context of the social, political and personal spheres influencing decision making and how it may impact on those who volunteer. Captain Jill Rutherford – Davies encapsulates many of the arguments and themes. Professional experience, time away from the "real job", the horror and brutality of war and the medical role to help all. This is coupled with a growing admiration by the British public for service personnel performing arduous and dangerous tasks in a difficult environment and finally, but very importantly, the personal support families give to the deploying individual.

When 207 returned from OP TELIC 4 in the late summer of 2004 many individuals, for a variety of reasons, left the unit. They had "Done their bit" and "Got their medal", the culmination of their TA career. But a hard core of seasoned veterans remained, and these individuals would form the foundations on which a new 207 would be built in preparation for not 'if' the unit was to deploy but 'WHEN'.

In 2005 the Unit enjoyed an "easy" Annual Camp in Penhale, Cornwall. Good weather, adventurous training and watching the RAF search and rescue helicopters practise retrieving casualties from a rock face were the highlights. The following year's Annual Camp was back in a soldiering mode by proving medical support for 102 Logistical Brigade on exercise Griffin Focus and more specifically a Relief in Place for our regular counterpart 34 Field Hospital. Relief in Place, or

RiP as it is known, means taking over the effective running of a hospital and providing care and administration whilst the hospital remains fully operational, it should be as seamless a transition as possible. The experienced staff relished the exercise but not the Scottish weather. The hospital and staff accommodation was all under canvas and the weather was gale force winds and rain for the majority of the exercise. For newer members on 207 this was their first experience of field conditions, leaking tents, damp clothes and washing with hot water from a 'Puffing Billy'[49]. After a week, the unit moved to Garelochead on the West coast of Scotland, for a week of further training. The abiding memory of this camp, for those who attended, were the midges, grey clouds coming in waves of trillions to feed on the poor English soldiers with relish.

The post OP TELIC era created certain problems which had to be resolved to maintain the viability of the unit. The unit was finding it difficult to keep up with recruitment to replace those who were leaving. In this era of continuing operations recruitment was specialist specific, as time would not allow for the development of these clinical skills. This significantly narrowed the scope for potential recruits, as what was required, were trained individuals who could, after a short period of militarisation, be sent into an operational environment. Trauma medical and nursing staff and ITU specialist were at a premium but were essential elements for any deploying unit. Captain Kevin Thornley the new Regimental Operational Support Officer (ROSO) set about forging links with the local NHS trusts and actively targeting these professional groups for recruitment and enlisting several key medical staff who would deploy to Afghanistan.

A recession was under way and health care Trusts were not easily persuaded to allow their senior staff to engage with the TA particularly as they had their own targets to meet. The new Commanding Officer, Colonel Robin Jackson, took the opportunity afforded by the Centenary of the TA in 2008 to host a dinner at The Imperial War Museum North in Salford, the guest speaker being the then Secretary of Health Alan Johnson MP. The invited guests were principally the senior executives and clinical staff of all the NHS Trusts in the North West. In his speech

---

49 The M67 water heater or 'Puffing Billy' was well known throughout the British Army for its unpredictable behaviour when being lit. Eyebrows where commonly lost by the person lighting it. It was retired in 2010 after many decades of providing 'clean' hot oily water.

he emphasised the role of the TA, particularly the medical element and the benefits to all parties by the individual joining and being prepared to do service. The other very significant break with tradition aimed at developing a partnership role with the NHS was the appointment of Felicity Goodey CBE, the Chair of University Hospital of South Manchester NHS Foundation Trust in 2009 as 207's Honorary Colonel The first "civilian" to accept this role.

It would be misleading to give the impression that recruitment was focused entirely on senior staff such as consultants and senior clinical nurses. Throughout the NHS the roles of carers had become more defined and following nationally recognised training Health Care Assistants (HCA) became the bedrock of care on all wards. Within the TA they were set to replace the CMT in all hospital clinical areas. Because of their hands on caring role they were badged QARANC. The motivation to join the TA however transcends professional barriers and encompasses an array of emotions and personal considerations. Mr Steve Hawes outlines many of the dilemmas individuals had, knowing they were seeking mobilisation to a war zone. His account also outlines the obstacles and hurdles he had to overcome and personal sacrifices he had to make, to ensure his aim was achieved; to mobilise with 207.

When the regional recruitment team came to speak to our registrars in the Emergency Department at the University Hospital of South Manchester I was the consultant taking their teaching session. None of the registrars were interested but I immediately realised that I had to volunteer. I didn't vocalise this at the time because it was a big decision which I knew I had to discuss with my wife and family and it wasn't until several weeks later that I responded. My motivation had a number of aspects which I found difficult to disentangle. The first was that I felt that if I had any skills which could help in treating our injured servicemen in Afghanistan then I had a duty to offer these, particularly considering the huge sacrifice many of them were making. The second was that the military system of trauma care was obviously far in advance of the NHS model at that time and I wanted to learn about it. The third was that if Camp Bastion was indeed the busiest trauma centre in the world with the best results then I just wanted to be part of it.

I had to pass a 3 day selection process to join the TA in York and then in the 12 months before deploying to Camp Bastion I had go on 2 x 2 week courses for Professionally Qualified Officers, one in York and the second at Sandhurst. I was commissioned as a Major in recognition of my civilian status as a Consultant in Emergency Medicine. After this came several more weeks of both military and clinical training including weekends and training nights which meant I had to use up half my annual leave in each of 2 consecutive leave years before deploying with 207 in September 2010. Amongst many things it has certainly been the highlight of my professional career and I have no regrets. In addition, the NHS has developed a system of major trauma centres since I have returned. My hospital has been chosen as one of them and my experiences in Afghanistan have undoubtedly helped me enormously in the management of a significant number of patients since my return.

Major Steve Hawes RAMC

At the start of 2009 new rumours began to circulate that 207 was to deploy again possibly to Afghanistan and in the autumn of that year the unit was formally given notice that it would be deployed on OP HERRICK.

When looked at on a map Afghanistan is a vast, land locked mass that is boarded to the west by Iran, to the north by three old Soviet states (Turkmenistan, Uzbekistan, Tajikistan) to the south and east by Pakistan and a small mountain pass border with China to the north east. But if you look a little closer you will find a society that reflects the diversity of the various invaders who have settled in Afghanistan over millennia making it their home.

Afghanistan's strategic location has over the years brought it to the attention of many expanding empires. Alexander the Great passed through on his way to conquer India and in the 19th century Russia and Britain played out their imperial games using Afghanistan as a very large pawn. She started the 20th century relatively peacefully, escaped the trauma of the First and Second world wars by remaining neutral but was to engage in its third war with Britain in 1919. In 1978 a communist coup in Afghanistan followed a year later by the Soviet invasion bought her back on to the world stage with the USA replacing Britain as Russia's opponent. The Soviet Union withdrew from Afghanistan in 1989. The same year saw the fall of the Berlin Wall which heralded the breakup of the Soviet Union and the end of the cold war. The USA's interest (and that of the world) waned in Afghanistan; she became just another failed state ruled by a hard line Islamic group known as the Taliban. And so it may have remained if not for the events of 11 September 2001 (9/11) which would set Afghanistan on a collision course with the USA and her allies and plunge her into a cycle of violence from which she is still to emerge.

The rise of the Taliban movement in Afghanistan, formed by a group of Islamic scholars, initially added some stability in a country devastated by occupation and civil unrest. Their strict and narrow view of Islam alienated them from many other Afghan communities and Islamic sects. Afghanistan had slipped from international view, the Taliban being just another group of despots. Events in other political spheres dominated the British Army. International on-going involvement in Bosnia, Kosovo and Sierra Leone, coupled with the long established threat of Irish Republicans stretched the now reduced numbers of troops available following the defence 'Options for Change' review in the early 1990s.

The rise of terrorist organisations, such as Al Qaeda, linked to the Islamic faith, was causing concern. British soldiers serving in Bosnia came across heavily armed and well trained fighters, many from Afghanistan, Pakistan and Arab countries who had come to support and fight for the oppressed Muslim minority in Bosnia. Osama bin Laden a veteran of the Muhjaden in Afghanistan planned and initiated attacks which were to bring the threat of Islamic terrorism to a global stage. Attacks in Africa and the Middle East often against Embassies, tourist or commercial interest of International companies led to significant casualties and a heightening of awareness. It was not however until the 9/11 attack on the USA that decisive action was taken. The USA considered the unprovoked attack as an act of war. In a gesture of radical Muslim solidarity, the Taliban refused to hand over bin Laden. The response of the USA and her allies, specifically the UK, was to initiate air and missile attacks on bin Laden's terrorist organisation including Al Qaeda training camps in Afghanistan. 207, as noted in the previous chapter, were on Annual Camp in Inverness when the events of 9/11 unfolded. Those who witnessed the events of that day may have thought that a war was coming but few would have envisaged that 207 would be deployed to both Iraq and Afghanistan within a decade.

Even before official confirmation of deployment was received, Colonel Jackson and his Command Team started to select individuals from within the unit who were going to be appropriate to the deployment. The unit entered an intense period of training, not just military, but medical as well. Many of the courses were familiar to members of the NHS as they would undertake them as part of their professional training, such as Advanced Life Support (ALS) and Acute Illness Management (AIM). Others were unique to military medicine such as the Military Operational Surgical Training (MOST). One course that several unit members undertook (both clinical and non-clinical) was the Trauma Risk Management (TRiM). All units now have TRiM trained personnel, from Lance Corporal upwards, whose role it is to help identify individuals who may be experiencing difficulties after a traumatic incidence.

Training for individuals hoping to be deployed was proceeding with gusto as the Command Team went to the Headquarters of 16 Air Assault Brigade at Colchester in January 2010 for their initial briefing from the infantry brigade they would be supporting. The Team comprised of;

Colonel Robin Jackson (Commanding Officer)

Lieutenant Colonel Kerry Trow (Senior Nursing Officer)

Lieutenant Colonel Eric Hunter (Officer Commanding the Rear Party)

Lieutenant Colonel Nick Medway (Trauma Nurse Coordinator)

Major Eddy Hardaker (Training Major who would deploy as 2IC)

Major Simon Davies, (Regular Nursing Officer who would deploy as the Emergency Department head of department)

Warrant Officer Class 1 (Regimental Sergeant Major) Scott Ferris

Major Mick Thompson Regimental Admin Officer and Captain Kevin Thornley ROSO also accompanied the team as they would have an integral part to play in administratively mobilising the troops and ensuring families and employers were informed of developments.

The briefing delivered by Brigadier Chiswell and his staff was upbeat but acknowledged the inherent difficulties and dangers of taking over Task Force Helmand. 16 Air Assault were very familiar with Afghanistan, this being their fourth deployment, they were not complacent and their professional assessment of the situation provided a considerable guidance as to how military operations would unfold in the coming year. Significant in this appraisal was that following a draw down in operations in Iraq the USA was deploying a large number of troops, a surge, to Afghanistan. Many of these new troops would be co-located in Helmand Province with British Forces and it was anticipated that the fighting would be taken to the Taliban and ground won would be occupied by the new forces, which had not always been the case in the past. The Taliban would not give up easily and an increase in the casualty rate was anticipated with obvious ramifications for the medical services. The Role 3 Medical Facility, the hospital at Camp Bastion would remain under British Command but would be jointly staffed by British and American personnel.

In late July of 2010 mobilisation papers for unit members began to drop through letter boxes. Two members of the unit (Major Charles Rowland and WO2 (RQMS) Kevin Duffy) deployed in September in order to prepare the way for the RiP planned for early October.

A military hospital, like any civilian hospital, is heavily reliant on the logistical elements that support it; chefs to feed it, drivers to move it and engineers to keep it supplied with power. On Bastion these support services would be provided by other units and civilians therefore 207 logistical elements would not be required to deploy. This did not mean however they did not provide important support to their deploying comrades. They formed the nucleus of what is referred to as the Rear Party and their first task was to ensure those deploying were in the right place at the right time. They also provide invaluable support during the Hospital's final exercise at Strensall. Not all members of the unit deployed with the main body and some did not stay for the full duration of the tour and it was the rear party that ensured these people departed the UK or arrived back in Manchester safely. Thankfully another task of the rear party, dealing with casualties among the deployed unit members, did not have to be actualised. On Friday 24 September 2010 members of 207 came together at the Old Trafford Depot now titled Sir William Coates House and like so many of their predecessors, said good bye to families and friends and set out for foreign fields. Many past members of the unit also came to wave the unit off and shared an odd joke with the newest members of the 207 family.

First stop was RTMC Chilwell for medicals, assessments and kit issue. Two members of the unit succumbed to medicals, which had a deflating

Figure 75 Tommy Willis shares a cheeky joke with Corporal Steve Booth and the newest member of 207 to deploy, Private Chrissy Barwick

effect on the rest. As they packed to go home the rest prepared for the combat fitness assessment. This eight mile walk was, without doubt, the single, most dreaded part of the Chilwell process, particularly 'THAT HILL!!' that had exhausted so many previous victims. 207 were no different and there was an anguished wait to see if any unit members would be rejected. None were and after a sad farewell to those who would not be travelling on, the rest reported to the QM's for kit issue.

Next stop was Lydd for OPTAG, here for the first time 207 came in to contact with some of the infantry soldiers they were going to support. The common comment from the more mature TA members was 'how young they were' and for those who had deployed before a wonder if these young men knew what was about to happen. As the unit departed Lydd there was an unusually farewell of 'we hope we never see you again' from 207 members to the young infantry soldiers they had grown to know over the previous few days.

The last port of call before leaving the UK was the Army Medical Services Training Centre (AMSTC) at Strensall near York. In a non-descript warehouse on Towthorp camp the AMS boasts a unique training facility, a hospital simulator whose equipment and layout closely mirrors that of the Role 3 Hospital on Bastion. Deploying hospital personnel are trained using scenarios (based on actual events) with role play casualties whose injuries graphically reflect those encountered for real in Afghanistan. Each deploying hospital is supported by directing staff and subject matter experts whose experience spans not just HERRICK but many other UK military operations. The whole training programme being brought together by the permanent staff who work long and hard to facilitate the hospital exercises, constantly looking for ways to improve and adapt the training delivered at AMSTC.

Each TA hospital prior to deployment undergoes three exercises at the Strensall training centre. At the time 207 was undergoing training the exercises consisted of Mission Specific Training (MST), Mission Specific Assessment (MSA) and the final exercise Mission Specific Evaluation (MSE). The initial MST was carried out by primarily 207 personnel, the MSA with 207 and some of the Regular and TA staff who would deploy and the final MSE with all the medical staff including the United States Naval Reserve troops who would be attached. It was at MSE that friendships and working relationships were forged; these formed the bed rock that allowed a group of people who had only known each other for a few days to take control of one of the busiest trauma centres in the world.

On 9 October 2010 the hospital squadron of OP HERRICK 13A began their journey to Camp Bastion from Brize Norton. The hospital personnel travelled on several different flights (known as chalks) and it would be three or four days before everyone arrived at Camp Bastion. On arrival in Afghanistan all personnel must undergo one final round of training at Camp Bastion prior to joining their units out on the ground. Reception Staging and Onward Integration (RSOI) is very similar to OPTAG with a mixture of practical sessions (which also aided acclimatisation) and the inevitable 'death by PowerPoint' presentations. RSOI staff had an ingenious way of maintaining interest by, in between presentations, showing episodes of the 'Inbetweeners'. As people completed their RSOI training they were filtered into the hospital to shadow those who they were to replace; the RiP had started.

The RiP is a challenging time for both units; the unit 'RiPing' out have worked long and hard hours (in the case of 34 Field Hospital for six months) providing medical care of the highest order to coalition troops, local nations and insurgents. Now the new hospital personnel had arrived, home was just a few short days away but were these new people "up to the job?" For the unit 'RiPing' in there was a feeling of excitement, their training was over, it was time to put it to good use. Feelings of excitement were tinged with that of apprehension particularly for those who had not deployed before. There was no safety net here, no rewind if anything when wrong, so that thought of 'am I up to the job?' could be found at the back of the mind of more than one of the incoming unit's personnel. Sergeant Phil Rodgers, who deployed as a wardmaster, describes his impressions of the RiP.

Arriving in Afghanistan with certain trepidations still forefront on my mind, it was consoling to find the incumbent Wardmasters from 34 Field Hospital equally familiar but at odds with the reporting systems. For my colleagues and I the handover was functional and informative although I sensed they couldn't wait to get the hell away and that being as they had struggled for months to come to terms with its demands that we poor unfortunates didn't have much chance. I felt a sense of being passed a baton they felt we were sure to drop! The "nemesis" of the Wardmasters life was "Reporting day". Every Thursday the major reports from the Hospital to the upper echelons had to be prepared in a relatively short period of time. The guys from 34 let it be known (I won't say boasted but it was close) that they had it off pat and down to about 6 hours. They must have known I liked a challenge.

Sergeant Phil Rodgers

Bastion, which is easily the size of a small town, is the home to thousands of people from all over the world. Troops, as you would expect, from the USA, UK and Denmark but also from countries you might not expect such as Georgia and Estonia. The military contractors are civilians who work alongside the military on many essential tasks and account for a considerable proportion of the camp population. These multi-national organisations employ people from the four corners of the globe as well as local Afghans. Feeding this small town is a mammoth task and as well as access to the cook houses, with their huge selection from roast dinners to corned beef 'butties', the British Soldier (and anyone else who happens to be passing) has access to various other eateries from the Expeditionary Force Institutes (EFI) to Pizza Hut. Whilst 207 were in Afghanistan the EFI (which is the in theatre arm of the Navy, Army, and Air Force Institutes (NAAFI)) underwent an upgrade resulting in the existing shop and coffee bar being extended to provide a further coffee bar (which would give any of the high street coffee shops a run for their money), and a gaming area where computer football games seemed to be the order of the day. Things did get slightly surreal when Pizza Hut displayed a phone number announcing that they would now take telephone orders, which would have been great if it wasn't for the fact UK troops' did not have access to non-military phones.

Figure 77 Pictured in the Emergency Department (ED) at Bastion, Major Steve Hawes with his American Navy counterpart Captain Ed Turner

There was a huge determination pervading the whole hospital structure both clinical and non-clinical. It was not so much a "can do" attitude but a WILL DO one. Whatever could be done would be done.

Major Steve Hawes RAMC

The hospital at Bastion from the outside is nothing special to look at but its unimposing exterior hides an extraordinary facility whose collective aim is to provide medical treatment second to none anywhere in the world. Most people on entering the building for the first time are surprised and often comment on how much it looks and feels like 'a normal hospital'. It is however in many ways unique, after all not many UK hospitals can boast not one but two Computerised Tomography (CT) scanners. Corporal Sykes describes what it is like to be a radiographer at the Role 3 Medical Treatment Facility (MTF) on Camp Bastion.

I had previously deployed on HERRICK 10 over the hectic summer of 2009 and it was very obvious that the equipment we had was not coping well with the frantic workload that we encountered. For the first time a consultant radiologist had deployed and this lead to requesting an Urgent Operational Requirements (UOR) for an uplift in equipment.

During HERRICK 10 the CT scanner had failed several times seriously reducing the diagnostic capability of the department. For Camp Bastion Radiology department it was imperative that we had two 64 slice Computerised Tomography (CT) scanners.

In little over a year these UORs were commissioned and up and running just over a month before 207's arrival. This was indeed a

major achievement for all concerned and a much needed boost for the deployed Med Group. The department had also taken delivery of three mobile DARTs, digital x-ray equipment that were more robust and had a better all-round performance than the previous Dragon digital mobiles, once again a welcome working advantage. The scene was set for a busy, high intense deployment.

As a deployment we began hitting the ground running. The radiology team had been increased in manpower to include three UK radiographers and two US personnel. This was a huge improvement from three UK radiographers on Herrick 10. The team also included a second consultant radiologist from the US.

Once a casualty's treatment has begun in the form of a primary survey, the usual treatment pattern includes a chest and pelvic x-rays for instant assessment, an image appears in three seconds allowing the doctors and surgeons to quickly assess whether the casualties treatment could incorporate a CT scan or go straight to the Operating Theatre (OR), a great advantage.

If CT was required then the speed with which the treatment was administered was quite astounding. Every second is vital for the casualty. As part of the team dealing with a casualty, we would supervise their transfer onto the scan table, connected to the intravenous contrast dye, their positioning on the table and the arrangement of the relevant attached medical equipment so the movement of the table prior and during the scan was not interfered with. This process was finely tuned to around eight minutes from start to finish. The actual scan of the casualty took just nine seconds for the whole body.

The consultant radiologists were on hand to provide 'Hot Reporting' giving the surgeons vital information regarding triage and the surgery required. This method of treatment cannot be replicated anywhere in the world in such casualty volume. It is indeed a unique environment in which to work and be clinically challenged and pushed to your maximum limit of your own personal radiographic capabilities.

The incidences of casualties would more often than not arrive in high numbers especially if the casualties had been involved with Improvised Explosive Devices (IEDs). This would create a very high intense workload; the radiology team had to work together playing their part in what is the ultimate team game - the attempt to keep the casualty alive.

As CT scans would continue you would find yourself in the OR providing follow up x-rays or Image Intensifier requests for orthopaedic pinning's. Intensive Therapy Unit would again be requesting chest x-rays for various injuries and to check many of the inserted lines which both help monitor and keep the patient alive. As a radiographer you had to be at the top of your game constantly for every eventuality you were called upon to perform.

Personally having now deployed on two tours in quick succession the work becomes addictive in every sense. You feel clinically fulfilled at having done your job in the most extreme of environments. Providing your skills and motivation in order to help our troops out on the ground so that they know there is a collection of medics back in Bastion that will be there for them in every eventuality.

Corporal David Sykes

Figure 78 Corporal David Sykes sat at one of the CT scanner terminals

Like Radiology, the biomedical science laboratory, far from being the remote department hidden way somewhere in the bowels of most NHS hospitals, is 'in the thick of it' and it most important commodity is blood.

Severe lacerated shell wound of the left thigh, and fracture of the femur, admitted to dressing station with tourniquet and Thomas splint applied. Intravenous injection of one pint 5% gum and 4% sodium bicarbonate produced a slight improvement in the pulse. A robust infantryman, buried by a shell, offered some blood, but turned out to belong to Group II, and had to be rejected. A slightly wounded corporal, Group IV, volunteered, and a pint of his blood was transfused without difficulty by the syringe method. Some improvement was noted, and the patient was warmed up and sent on. He died just before reaching the casualty clearing station. We have since thought that if this case had been given more blood, and allowed to warm up longer in the dressing station, he might have survived the long ambulance journey.[42]

Captain N M Guiou, Canadian Army Medical Corps 1918

The importance of blood in the treatment of trauma cases is nothing new as the quote above shows; in fact Captain Guiou highlights two of the greatest factors that can mean the difference between life and death for the trauma casualty; blood loss and hypothermia. Today we tend not to ask other casualties to donate blood and the physicians of the Great War would be truly amazed at the volume of blood that is transfused into a single casualty in Afghanistan. Blood is best used fresh and has a limited shelf life. The majority of blood used by the UK military medical service in Afghanistan comes from the UK. Corporal Steve Booth describes some of the problems that transporting blood over vast distances can cause and give an insight into how blood products are used in Afghanistan.

It is the case that between 40-60% of all trauma victims (civilian) die because they lose too much blood before they get to hospital so that doctors are not able to work their magic. In the military context the figure was higher.

In the Falkland's war blood was sent by sea prior to the troop landings and unfortunately had all expired before the troops landed so the entire supply was from fighting troops when not in action.

Though distances are comparable blood supply is now flown into theatre.

The present system provides blood and plasma on the helicopter (MERT) that picks the casualty up at the site of the incident. This supply of emergency O negative blood and AB plasma is sufficient to maintain the casualty to the role 3 hospital at Bastion.

More emergency O negative blood and plasma is made ready at ED ready for the arrival of the patient. A system is in place such that the laboratory can then supply large quantities of blood and plasma through A&E and the operating theatre until the doctors and surgeons are able to control the bleeding.

A further supply is provided for ICU to the point that the casualty is evacuated, usually within 24-36 hours after injury.

A further supply is sent with the patient for use during the transport back to the UK.

All blood and blood products are maintained at the correct temperatures with the correct documentation at all times to exactly the same standard that is required under UK legislation.

Blood and plasma is supplied from the UK several times a week so the blood donors in the UK are routinely saving the lives of the soldiers in Afghanistan.

Corporal Steve Booth

The majority of blood products used in Afghanistan are issued by the biomedical science laboratory at the Role 3 MTF on Camp Bastion. Corporal Booth describes the way blood products are made available to the medical team from the casualty being picked up by the MERT to their return to the UK. For each trauma casualty the laboratory staff must ensure not only the compatibility of all blood products with the patient but that a robust supply is maintained. One of the ways of ensuring a regular supply is to take blood from your own troops as Corporal Booth explain

Platelets, a critical part of keeping casualties alive, are supplied from the UK. Once produced in the UK they have a maximum life of 5 days, thus usually 3-4 when they arrive in theatre and as a result

were always in short supply and would run out if not supplemented. For this reason troops are asked to volunteer to be part of a donor panel and be available to donate platelets when there is a need.

Donors are screened in UK before deployment and in theatre. This involves day long sessions once or twice per month.

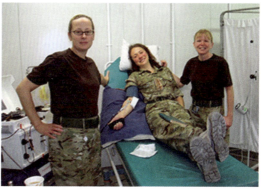

Figure 79 The blood donor panel in action, Majors Rosalind (Ros) Peel (right) and Angie Nicholls (left), on the bed Captain Beth Hall Thompson one of the General Duties Medical Officers. This was probably one of the few times Beth was able to 'put her feet up' during her tour of duty.

When platelets are needed then a 6 strong team set up in the hospital and call forward people from the panel. Each unit takes 2 hours to obtain and there is a capacity to take 2 at any one time. The team was in action most weeks in the 3 months I was there. The team would run sessions that would last from 6-8 hours on average to 24 hour on one occasion. This job was extra to their other duties and always had laboratory staff supporting.

Unique to Afghanistan is the use of fresh whole warm blood that was given to casualties just prior to evacuation, 2-4 units. This requires a unit of blood being taken from a donor and immediately being transfused into the casualty. This was also carried out by the donor team, invariably took place in the early hours of the morning and required some degree of alacrity on the part of the laboratory staff on duty to carry out testing and processing in a very short time scale.

To give exact blood usage is militarily sensitive but an example of one of the most serious cases was, a young soldier was caught up in an explosion and received just short of 150 units of blood, plasma, cryoprecipitate (plasma with concentrated clotting factors) and platelets in a 12 hour period. The soldier was evacuated back to the UK and survived.

The logistics of maintaining adequate supplies of blood and blood products is immensely complex and requires the ability to respond at very short notice to supply demands beyond anything previously experienced.

Corporal Steve Booth

There are a number of roles within a military hospital that would not be found in the NHS such as the wardmasters, the 'front of house' personnel and the Trauma Nurse Coordinator (TNC).

Under the command of the RSM the 'front of house' personnel were made up of CMTs and pioneers and had one of the most difficult jobs in the hospital. They provided security for the hospital; the mere presence of Staff Sergeant Melia would calm any troublesome situation that occasionally arose. They coordinated the unloading of the casualties and, perhaps the hardest part of their job, they cared for the dead before there repatriation to the UK.

As a regular soldier this wasn't my first operational tour, it was my tenth but my first with the TA. I was originally deploying to work as a wardmaster but was able to wangle a move outside to the front of house staff for a little daylight and fresh air, some days I wish I had stayed inside though. It was always busy with casualties coming into the hospital at all times of the day and the only time there was a lull was on a Thursday night. I also worked in the mortuary which wasn't a particularly nice job to have. We were fiercely protective of the department especially when it came down to dressing the coffins for any repatriations. The flag had to be perfect and no matter how many times it had to be done, nobody got stressed even though sometimes we were absolutely shattered, we felt it was the least we could do for one of our own who had given the ultimate sacrifice and we were proud to do it. The tour went by very quickly (probably because we didn't really get the time to get bored) and before you knew it we were on our way back to the UK. I enjoyed my time immensely working with 207 who I consider to be some of the most professional people I have ever had the pleasure to work with this has encouraged me to join 207 since leaving the Regular Army in June 2012.

Staff Sergeant Paul Melia RAMC

Figure 80 Taken outside the hospital entrance, Staff Sergeant Paul Melia (right), Major Simon Davies (Centre) and RSM Harris of 16 Medical Regiment

For some members of the unit this was not only their first tour it was also the first time they had worked within a hospital and they took every opportunity to experience the military medical system to the full.

It was my first deployment and I found myself doing the role of the Ops Room Wardmaster. As a non-medical person I found the job difficult at times for no other reason than I was not familiar with some of the medical terminology and seeing some of the injuries sustained. For the majority of time it was a very busy job but occasionally I found time to help out the AELO and her team. One evening I assisted them in setting up an aircraft ready for the CCAST team to take our wounded soldiers back to the UK. This task was always carried out very late at night/early hours of the morning so although I was tired at the end of it I felt satisfied in what I had achieved.

Staff Sergeant Julie Misell AGC(SPS)

The role of the Wardmaster is one of the oldest within a military hospital and the basic responsibilities have not changed, that of administration and collating the hospital reports and returns. They also help soldiers make contact with family and friends back home, in the past by providing pencil and paper, today by arranging telephone to locations around the world. The Wardmasters would normally be located in the hospital's HMC but in Afghanistan they work between the Operational Room (the Ops Room) of the Medical Group and the Hospital Reception. Sergeant Rodgers worked alongside Staff Sergeant Misell in the Ops Room. When casualties where expected they were amongst the first to know.

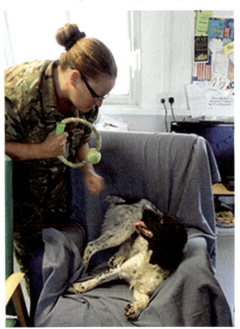

Figure 81 Staff Sergeant Julie Misell with one of the regular visitors to the hospital. Military working dogs would attend the hospital both to visit patients and as patients themselves

Every day the SO2, our very own Major Ray Gregson later in the tour, would chase the current status of all UK casualties over the phone. In fact the phone never seemed to stop ringing with enquiries from all and sundry. Our eyes were firmly fixed on the Casualty board next to the "Watch keeper" on our left hand side which liaised and worked alongside the Hospital Reception (HR). This showed us casualties occurring in the field following contacts. There always seemed to be a respectful hush when serious allied casualties were incoming like everyone was holding their breath. On the few occasions, with the deaths of UK casualties, the room would be seemingly silent and reflective almost tinged with a hint of sadness as we knew we would be attending another memorial service soon, another two minutes silence, another young life lost.

Sergeant Phil Rodgers

The military medical facilities in Afghanistan are, by the nature of the injuries occurring, at the forefront of trauma care management. New methods of treating casualties are evolving through research as each case is systematically studied to see if valuable lessons can be learnt. Analysis of the nature of the injuries and how they were caused (for example Improvised Explosive Device, IED), is leading to improvements in personal protective equipment and the redesign of vehicles. The collator of this information in a hospital setting is the TNC.

I would describe the role of TNC as a "full on back room function" I was co-located with three US women in a portacabin type office with no natural light. Best described as an over-stocked corner shop, the room was packed with every conceivable US confectionary which were regularly resupplied in shipments from the US. There we spent 14 to 15 hours per day auditing all the clinical notes of trauma victims to gather information which may ultimately influence trauma care and military medicine. I soon came to realise that despite having no windows our "view" of the patient journey through Bastion was probably more complete than anyone else as we audited the journey from admission to transfer out.

I was allowed out of the office very regularly to act as scribe for the trauma teams at major trauma calls - this was at times harrowing but always a privilege - I felt very much a part of the trauma team and although I could never adequately convey the experience to someone who had not been there I will carry that vision of the dedication and care given to every trauma victim with me for the rest of my life.

Lieutenant Colonel Nick Medway

Colonel Medway makes mention of one of the most endearing memories of the Americans, their apparent addiction to processed sugar in all its conceivable forms. As each holiday period approached the amount and diversity of the candy available seemed to grow exponentially. Each of the holidays we shared with the Americans (Halloween, Thanksgiving and Christmas) introduced some joy and happiness in to an environment which was, at times, both sad and painful to endure. Thanksgiving was particularly memorable when one of the American liaison personnel, 'Doc' Curry, arrived at the hospital with turkey and all the trimmings for the on-duty staff. He repeated this on Christmas Day bringing steak at lunch time and turkey in the evening followed by an assortment of fruit pies. Local holidays were also celebrated and at Eid al Fitr (the end of Ramadan) some of the local people who were working for Task Force Helmand came to the hospital dressed in colourful traditional clothing bearing gifts for both staff and patient and in particular the children.

In November Bastion, as all other British Military Bases around the world, marked the loss of comrades in conflicts both past and present by the wearing of poppies and services of Remembrance. Prince William came on Remembrance Sunday and visited some of the patients before attending the service of Remembrance at the Bastion memorial. The day was made all the more sombre when, in the early hours of the morning, Ranger Aaron McCormick of the Royal Irish Regiment was killed. For those members of staff who could not attend the service Padre Hall held an evening service in St Luke's, the hospital chapel, where poppies and poppy crosses were laid on the alter.

I think it would be fair to say that the chaplain's role in the R3 (UK) Hospital, Camp Bastion, is a unique and privileged one - at least as far as chaplains are concerned in other organisations such as the NHS. It is unique and privileged role because with the blessing of the CO one has complete access to all the departments in the hospital, including ED and theatres, so long as one seeks the permission of the OC of each department. This means that one is at hand to minister both spiritually and pastorally to all those who come into each department, staff and injured alike. This includes the mortuary where a chaplain can minister to those who work under particularly difficult circumstances. But this access isn't something which is an expectation by the chaplain but one by the staff who find great comfort in a chaplain's presence, whether they are particularly religious or not. In my time as chaplain to the hospital I was designated a foot square box marked out on the floor outside the sluice room in ED where I could observe and pray for those who came into Bay 1, the bay where the most seriously injured came into. Of course one didn't spend ones time observing the injured but rather the staff to see if they had any particular issues resulting from the treatment of the terrible traumas that came through ED, and if so one could deal with this immediately. This could particularly be the case when injured children came in. Of course a chaplain should be on hand to pray and I found myself praying constantly during those traumatic moments in ED, as well as in theatres and ICU, and I was also on hand if prayers for the dying or the dead were needed, as they unfortunately were all too frequently.

I used to describe myself as someone who wandered around the place having cups of tea with some of the nicest people I have had the privilege to work with or encounter. The reality was somewhat more than just this, of course, and although I wasn't

Figure 82 Padre Ian Hall (left) and Padre Andy Earl taken outside the hospital chapel St Luke's

a medical person I certainly felt part of the team that made up the hospital, and an essential part of all that happened there. From a ministerial perspective it was probably the most challenging and yet the most rewarding experience I have ever had.

Padre Ian Hall

The Royal Army Chaplains Department has provided care, compassion and spiritual guidance to members of the Army since 1796 both in peace time and war. Each unit has its own chaplain and they could often be seen roaming the hospital carrying out their pastoral duties. Padre Hall, as he described above, would often 'pop in' to departments for a cup of tea and a chat. For those who required a more peaceful and quite place the doors of St Luke's were always open, and if Padre Hall was in, there would be a cup of tea and a biscuit from his secret stash. The hospital chaplain was not the only member of staff whose primary job was the soldier's welfare. The connection between the Order of St John's, the British Red Cross, and the British military can be traced back well over one hundred years. In 1910 Colonel

Coates formed the East Lancashire Branch of the British Red Cross Society and the Order of Saint John's connection was formalised in 1888 when it received its Royal Charter from Queen Victoria. Today this relationship takes the form of the St John and Red Cross Defence Medical Welfare Services (DMWS). When a field hospital deploys it takes with it members of the DMWS, in our case we had Penny and Jayne who quickly integrated into the fabric of the hospital. Although their role was to provide welfare to the British military patients, their care and compassion for the hospital staff was of great note and they were both held in great regard and affection by both patients and staff.

The hospital played host to many visitors over the four months 207 was there. From official visits such as Princes, British Government Ministers and American Secretaries of State to the more light hearted visitors such as the Hollywood film star Mark Wahlberg and football legend Stuart Pearce. But perhaps the biggest stir was caused not by a person but by a cup when the Premier League Trophy came to visit. Such excitement did it cause that the football mad radiographers gave it a CT scan to ensure it had not suffered unduly during its visit to Bastion.

Figure 83 Penny (left) and Jayne with Captain Michael Hughes and Staff Sergeant Andrew Higgins (right)

With the name of Manchester in our title, football rivalries were never far from the surface, and on Christmas Day a blue Father Christmas was seen at the hospital reception desk. Christmas Day was marked as being the only day when the hospital received no seriously injured casualties. The hospital was visited by no fewer than three Father Christmas' (red ones) and a gospel choir that filled the hospital corridors with the sound of Christmas carols. ITU had out shone the other departments by sporting a real Christmas tree which had been sent via the American postal service by one of the ITU nurse's relatives.

Figure 84 Corporal David Sykes with the HMC Father Christmas (Corporal Scott Jibson)

Figure 85 The Hospital Christmas Eve Carole concert. In the centre Colonel Robin Jackson to his left Private Chrissy Barwick and other members of the nursing staff

Colonel Jackson was keen to ensure that he had a viable unit to return to, that recruitment was enhanced and every member was valued. Although weekend training was reduced it maintained the traditional seasonal objective of ensuring bounty was achieved, coupled with hard work and fun. One of the most important roles of the rear party was to provide support to the families of those deployed. Major Mary Nixon the Unit Welfare Officer (UWO) did a splendid job in organising functions aimed at providing information and support. Children's parties and a Carol Service at Bury Parish Church helped promote a season of good will over-shadowed by events in Afghanistan. The making of a video of Christmas messages in which over 200 family members took part was perhaps the highlight and required all the IT skills of the

Media Officer, Captain Alan Bethell, to produce. In the afternoon of Christmas Day 207 unit members gathered in the welfare area of the hospital to watch the video and receive presents. Around the hospital as a whole there was an air of fun and joyfulness that was finished off by the sharing of a full turkey dinner (courtesy of 'Doc' Curry) by the on duty hospital staff.

> *Some of my worst inhibitions of going to war have resulted in the most treasured aspects in my life – I have gained a group of friends whose compassion and loyalty I will never forget*
>
> *Lieutenant Commander Cheryl C Ringer United States Navy, Medical Services Corps*

The holiday spirit that had flowed around the hospital on Christmas Day was swiftly replaced on Boxing Day by the realities of the conflict with American deaths along with several other seriously injured casualties. The year ended with a British fatality. Yet despite all the sadness and tragedy that invaded the hospital daily the spirit of the people who staffed it remained true to the eternal optimism of the military medic. People who had been strangers only a few months before had now formed strong bonds that would endure long after the deployment had ended.

It is often said that the conflict in Afghanistan is the bloodiest foreign conflict the British Army have been involved in since the Korean War in the early 1950s; the casualty figures certainly reflect this view. As a result of this the profile of the Army Medical Services (as well as those of the RAF and Navy) has been raised not just with the public but amongst the military services themselves. From the first attending medic on the ground, to the inflight medical treatment of the MERT that keeps casualties alive on route to the hospital. The onward journey home in the form of CCAST and MEDIVAC back to the UK and to the Royal Centre for Defence Medicine based at the Queen Elizabeth Hospital Birmingham. Once initial treatment is completed the long term support and rehabilitation provided by Headley Court and long after wars are forgotten, places like Broughton House[50] who continue to provide care for any ex-service personnel in need. The British

---

50 Broughton House which Sir William Coates help create during the Great War still exists today as a home for ex-service men and women continuing the work it was created for nearly 100 years ago.

military medical services and its partners can be justly proud of the support they provide to the British armed forces and their families.

During 207's time at the Role 3 Medical Treatment Facility on Camp Bastion this respect and affection for the medical services took many guises: From a simple hug to small gifts given to individual hospital personnel to letters address to all the hospital personnel. This chapter closes with one such letter.

THE 2ND BATTALION
THE PARACHUTE REGIMENT

THANK YOU

Thank You

To all the Staff in your dept. thankyou for looking after the injured Paratrooper's from the other day.

No amount of words will explain how greatful we are for your care.

From all the men in 2 Para It is a real comfort to know that you a only a heli. lift away. We take real comfort in knowing that we have such a good network of remarkable people that look after us in the way you do. Thanks for everything this week.

2 Para R.G.

Figure 86
Letter addressed to all hospital personnel on the last day of 207 (Manchester) Field Hospital's tour

Figure 87 207 (Manchester) Field Hospital's home coming parade, Bury, March 2011

The Future

I remember a chap called Mike Gregson. When I first joined, he was a Lance Corporal, he left about 2 – 3 years ago as a Warrant Officer. I always remember him saying at his leaving do: "You can't get bigger than 207, it will always outlive you". I didn't realise what he was saying at the time, but I do now.

Sergeant Vinny March

The individuals who continue to be associated with the TA, officer or soldier, remain the same, endeavouring to uphold the principles of service and looking to their collective history for inspiration and resolve. The unit or more precisely the medical unit now associated with Manchester has outlived many. History continues to be made though, which places the individual within the context of unit identity and gives substance to their achievement and service. Colonel Deepak Bhatnagar became the first 207 TA personnel to go on OP HERRICK, to Afghanistan in 2007. The Colonel led by example and set the standard for others to follow; he will always be the first though.

Throughout the century, individuals stand out; the Coates family and Commanding Officers such as Colonels Steele and Ollerenshaw who both had long associations with various Manchester Medical Units. However, it is the countless number of individuals of all ranks that have given their time to serve who ensure the collective memory of the unit. Mr Gregson is right, the individual may go but it is anticipated that the unit will continue to outlive us all.

The Manchester Medic has seen over a century of change. Medical units do not have Battle Honours, but it is certain that where fighting is taking place and casualties expected, a medic would be present. Their valour and dedication to their patient is evident in the number of Victoria Crosses bestowed on Army Medical Services personnel. There are countless numbers who just did their job and their only satisfaction was a job well done and surviving another day.

A generation bloodied in war, are intermixed with newer members of the unit with little appreciation of the demands of mobilisation. Since 2000 the situation with the on-going "war on terrorism" the unit and all the other TA Field Hospitals remain on a constant cycle of readiness for mobilisation. Individuals continue to go as relief for other medical units and at any given time 207 will probably have several TA personnel serving on operations.

This period of expectation to serve has had its own consequence. The TA and reservists in general have stepped up to the mark and have seen continual service in all operations of war. They have performed well, exceptionally in many instances. The positive consequence of this is expressed in the expectations which form the basis of Future Reserves 2020. Nationally as the size of the Regular Army decreases the reservist size will double to 30,000 and be given the equipment and training on par with the Regular Army.

This smaller Army will require fewer medics to look after it either at war or in peace. The individuals targeted now for recruitment are generally trained medical professionals or individuals who will enhance deployment, such as drivers and chefs. Throughout the 207's history the non-medical support soldier has in many ways epitomised the volunteer ethos but has now been marginalised. The few remaining in the unit have evolved and taken on roles not in keeping with their initial training as a Combat Medical Technician, WO2 Aneep Mandviwala being just one example. Initially joining the TA as an infanteer, transferring to the RAMC, trained as a CMT went on various deployments in that role but in his last deployment was utilised in his civilian capacity as an information technology expert. This situation is not uncommon and recognises the skills individuals bring with them. The utility and robustness of the CMT gave the Commanding Officer many options in the areas to which they could be deployed and used and it would be remiss of the Army Medical Services not to define a career pathway for this important group of volunteers. Under 2020 the size of the TA is to increase. Incorporating such talented people should be given thought, they want to work in a medical environment and looking at how modern hospitals function, specific roles would indicated. Similarly hospitals deployed rely on other arms to police, protect and help with labour duties, they also have a reliance on locally recruited nationals to clean and launder. Again we will not always be able to rely on such help and we need to re-build our own flexibility and utility

Clinical Governance specifies areas of clinical competence, which determine the area in which a health care professional can practice. Ordinarily this would not cause problems, however specifically on operations; this narrowing of professional scope leaves the Army with few options when they are faced with children, the elderly and pregnant women. Flexibility is required and it is often found in the career profiles of individuals who may not be current but have enough versatility and clinical memory to provide adequate care. The medical parameters the Army faces are not fixed, in fact they are extensive, models of recruitment and individual role assessment should reflect that concept otherwise a point will come, as history tells us that we are not fit for role. We are defining the war, but the war will define us.

Armies are expensive and as we live through another financial recession the Government has to address significant monetary shortfalls. The 2020 review emphasises that in expanding the TA it will no longer be an 'add on' but an integrated component of the army. The role of the TA should be one of complementary service with the Regular Army. If in the event of hostilities a regular doctor, nurse or store man is sent from their base feasibly they could be replaced by a TA volunteer. Most TA clinical staff would not require much training to take over the roles of their colleagues at Queen Elizabeth Hospital (military) Birmingham. Such roles have not been assessed and are reliant on a new way of looking at utility. You do however need a larger pool of individuals than is currently available to the TA. Another positive recommendation from the 2020 review is streamlining the present system and making it easier for ex-regulars to join the TA. History, unfortunately, has had a way of catching out the unprepared as Nichols and Rennell[43] point out that prior to both World Wars previous debilitating cuts in the TA Medical services left them few in numbers and bereft of medically trained individuals to instruct the newcomers. The present day TA has a small but significant pool of experienced individuals who need to be valued and encouraged to pass on their experiences. With the likelihood of deployments to purpose built hospital facilities finishing, following withdrawal from Afghanistan, recruiting individuals with an experience of contingency operation, hospitals under canvas will be invaluable. Major Tom Howell earlier alluded to that without this group; a unit will have to constantly re-learn all its past mistakes.

The last few decades have heralded advances in social equality. The class divide has to some extent been eroded. The Army though is socially unique in many ways in its behaviour code, work ethic and adherence to values, many would argue, not representative of the "modernisation process" going on in society at present. The Army extols its commitment to this process but still wrestles in how precisely it will come to terms with this. Retirement ages are going up particularly in the NHS. Personal fitness to enable a soldier to deploy may have to be considered on clinical role expectations. For example an anaesthetist working in a hospital full time would be able to deploy to that role or similarly take over a position to enable a regular to deploy. If retirement ages grow longer with increasing utility a TA pension plan maybe applicable. All are on-going issues that will be determined primarily on cost rather social expectations but should seek to enhance the concept of service in a modern age.

The TA with its increasing utilisation and integration into the large Army needs to be seen as an equal partner, to do that we need to constantly induct all individuals, as ex RSM Colin Gidman outlines

There's a certain code of behaviour and standard – a code of dress and behaviour you need to adhere to and part of the training is learning how to live in the Mess. If you get a posting to a regiment or you go with a regiment, you don't feel out of place. You know your barracks yourself, you don't embarrass your unit, you don't embarrass anyone else – because you know how to behave. You know there are certain rules you've got to obey, certain dress codes, and without those teachings ..... courses, really you haven't a clue. And that's part of the problem with a lot of training camps these days they haven't got the facilities we need for the size of the unit we are.

The constant reminder to uphold the principles of the Army requires 207's core values to be high. Individuals will serve their entire career in 207, perhaps over thirty years. This is unique to the TA as no regular medical soldier or officer would spend so long in one posting. The unit has to be its own auditor of standards and to do so as RSM Gidman points out you need the facilities and environment to do so on a regular basis otherwise standards will inevitably drop. This has proven difficult as many of the traditionally used training camps have now closed and even in those still open, the facilities of individual messing are invariably not available. Regular staff attached to the TA should be of the highest standard and look to enhance the TA rather than put ongoing obstacles in the way of individual or the units development.

The modernisation process has had a considerable impact on the National Health Service. The Army Medical Health Services have tried to mirror as far as practicable the changes seen in health care delivery. A prime example would be integration of care for the military into main stream NHS hospital. Health care management has also evolved and a new career based upon the principles of managerialism has developed. The regular army staff may aspire to this role within military hospitals, the TA has either to nurture individuals from within or try to recruit them. A senior administrative nurse will be difficult to recruit as under present conditions there is no defined role for such individuals, as they may not be clinically current and in the strictest terms not be recruitable or deployable.

Again it is about sensible recruiting looking at the wider picture. Certain individuals may no longer be able to deploy, but are invaluable in terms of training, organisation and mess duties and have a continuous role to keep the unit functioning.

Within the concept of health care managerialism the traditional roles of clinician, nurse have been reshaped. The manager can come from any given health care profession; indeed their background can be pure management. Within the Army and to a lesser extent the TA this has seen professions other than medicine take over senior roles within units. Colonel Kerry Trow L/QARANC became the first nurse to Command 207 Field Hospital and will invariably be followed by others as the Army seeks the right calibre of person not a cap badge.

Increasing educational requirements for healthcare professionals invariably means that once qualified most will possess a basic university degree. During the Cold War era, many professions were recruited and retained by the TA with the enticement of a Commission. This has now stopped, apart from doctors, dentists and physiotherapists. All newly qualified nurses will as an example come in as Soldier Nurse, becoming a Lance Corporal once qualified. Career pathways and promotion will be based on professional and military ability rather than time served. A decline in officers but a rise in the occupancy of the Sergeants' Mess is anticipated.

Recruiting and retention will remain a constant problem. The post script to mobilisation on OP TELIC 4 was that a core of people left the unit having "done their bit" leaving a significant man power hole of experienced staff. Replacing these individuals is proving difficult and may significantly influence the unit's capacity to mobilise in the future. The TA is in competition with many other external activities and is looking to attract individuals with very specific abilities. The process of recruitment and induction into the Army is failing many and again the principles underpinning the process will have to be continually monitored so as not to cut off this source of new blood that every unit depends upon.

Word of mouth continues to be the best form of recruiting method. This implies that the initiator is enjoying their TA service. Training that is enjoyable, demanding and meets the expectations of the individual will always encourage people to stay and others to join. Foreign travel is also another bonus. Training with the Regular Army in Canada or Kenya, expeditions to Morocco or Norway organised by the unit all encourage the individual and boost the profile of the unit. The 2012 annual camp to Sennelager, Germany is a welcome return to overseas training.

With fewer individuals required to staff smaller hospital units, administrative collaboration is often referred to, combining the Manchester and Liverpool Field Hospitals and having a single North West Hospital is an option. It however would be inconceivable that a geographical area the size of Greater Manchester should not be able to provide sufficient individuals to staff a smaller established Field Hospital. Retaining a recruiting footprint in local areas is important. 2010 saw the closure of Blackburn Squadron followed by Ashton in 2012 both in their time were vibrant squadrons (or detachments). The 2020 review gives a commitment to modernise TA Centres, the future must include plans to utilise what is left to enhance the future role and be an incentive to the new recruit.

The TA also has to regain its association with its local community and the population as a whole. With so many individuals serving with regular troops, and TA members being injured or unfortunately killed, the profile of all the armed forces particularly the Army has risen with the general public. The local population, from which the TA was initially recruited, is often alienated, kept apart from its activities which are only witnessed on Remembrance Sunday. 207 (Manchester) Field Hospital has to re-kindle its association. Wearing proudly the Manchester Eagle would be an appropriate beginning.

TA centres "The Drill Hall" were often regarded as community centres where civic receptions, parties and even weddings could take place, this isn't the case anymore, where security dominates and Health and Safety defines reasonable risk. Opening up the centres would bring back communal association and generate a civic wellbeing, increasing local and national affiliation to the TA and the Army as a whole.

The Manchester Medics should be proud of their heritage. A century has passed since the TA was initiated and the concluding remarks from Colonel Elder's History of 207 in 1977 are as fitting a conclusion to this history, as they remain as pertinent today as they did then:

The importance and relevance of the Unit is greater than ever before and hopefully this short history will serve not only as a reminder of our past but a stimulus to our future.

Figure 88 Manchester Eagle

Figure 89 207 (Manchester) Field Hospital Freedom of the City of Manchester

The Manchester Medic Post Script

Saturday 22 October 2011.

The sun shone on a bright Manchester day as 207 Field Hospital marched into Albert Square led by the band of the Lancashire Artillery (V). A large crowd had assembled, family and friends but also many ordinary people keen to show their appreciation. Already assembled were a squad of "Veterans" former members of the unit who on this special occasion exemplified the continuity of service which the Medical Corps have given.

Under a marque and saluting platform the dignitaries from the City of Manchester congregated .The Deputy Lord Mayor Elaine Boyes made a speech commenting on the valuable role these local medics performed and commending them for their professionalism and dedication. Sir Howard Bernstein, Chief Executive read out the citation which bestowed upon 207 Field Hospital the Freedom of the City of Manchester.

Colonel Kerry Trow, Commanding Officer of 207 (Manchester) Field Hospital (Volunteers), in his acceptance speech emphasised the role of the medic:

"We are soldiers first, healthcare professionals second. The satisfaction from doing our jobs well, providing first class care for British soldiers, is the only reward we seek. So, to be honoured in this way with the Freedom of the City by the Council and the people of Manchester is a huge privilege. It makes us enormously proud and is one of the most important events in the history of 207 (Manchester) Field Hospital (Volunteers)."

Following an inspection of the troops by the Deputy Lord Mayor, 207 exercised their newly acquired right to march through the streets of Manchester. With the band playing and a swagger in their step the Manchester Medics set off on a circular route down Deansgate.

The new leading the old, the crowds applauding, the Manchester Medics were very much on familiar territory.

Appendix 1 Colonel Sir William Coates

On 14 June 1960 Colonel Sir William Coates reached the grand age of 100 years young. In celebration the following short biography was published.

Sir William Coates

K.C.B. (Civ.), C.B.E., V.D., T.D., C.St.J., F.R.C.S., D.L.

(Officer de la Couronne, Belgium)

Sir William Coates, who is due to have his hundredth birthday on the 14th June, 1960, came to Manchester in 1884 having qualified at the London Hospital, and began medical practice in Moss Side. He took into partnership Mr A.G. Andrews, F.R.C.S. and Dr C J Dabbs, which partnership was dissolved in 1913. While in Moss Side, Sir William attended St Clement's Church, Greenheys, the Rector at that time being the Rev. William Robinson.

In 1891 Sir William came to live at Ingleside, Whalley Range, where he still resides, the Rev. Hope being Rector of St Margaret's Church when he came. Since then he has attended St Margaret's, in later years with his wife and family until 1953 when he lost his sight became otherwise incapacitated and unable to walk to Church. He has followed closely, however, the fortunes of St Margaret's and continues to do so. For many years he read the lessons at the morning service.

In 1902 at the invitation of Sir John William Maclure who lived in Whalley Road, Sir William became a Trustee of St Margaret's, an appointment which he held for half a century, being the Chairman of Trustees for the greater part of the time.

Sir William was actively engaged in his professional work until he was over 90 years of age. He continued general practice throughout and in addition started a consulting practice at 17 Market Street in 1905, moving to 17 St John St. in 1935. He was appointed Secretary of the Manchester Medical Society about 60 years ago and later became President. He was Secretary of the National Medical Union which was formed in an endeavour to counter Lloyd George's National Health

Scheme under the Chairmanship of Mr G. A. Wright.

Apart from his prominence in the medical profession, Sir William had many other interests.

In 1885 he became Acting Surgeon, 20th Lancashire Rifle Volunteer Corps, now 8th (Ardwick) Battalion, The Manchester Regiment Territorial Army, and in 1886 was instrumental in forming the Manchester Volunteer Medical Staff Corps, being appointed to command in 1887. In 1900 he raised a special Bearer Company for the South African War.

He raised the greater part of the money which provided for the building of the Volunteer Royal Army Medical Corps Headquarters in Upper Chorlton Road, in 1904. On ceasing to command the Corps in 1908 he was appointed Assistant Director Medical Services 42nd East Lancashire Division Territorial Force and in 1914 Honorary Colonel of the R.A.M.C. units. In the same year he became A.D.M.S. Western Command, in which appointment he was responsible for assisting the D.D.M.S. in the formation and control of all hospital in Western Command throughout the 1914-1918 war. Although his office was in Chester, he was allowed to live at home and so was able to keep together a little of his professional work.

Sir William was a member of Lord Haldane's Committee at the War Office in 1906 and 1907 which considered the formation of the Territorial Force to follow the Volunteers. He was a member of the East Lancashire Territorial Association from its inception in 1907 and was Chairman from 1925 and 1946, following Lord Brackley and Sir Frank Forbes Adam in the appointment.

In 1910 he organised and formed the British Red Cross Society in East Lancashire under the Presidency of Lady Brackley (later Countess of Ellesmere) and later became Chairman and County Director. He was a member of the Joint V.A.D. Council in London, County Controller of V.A.D.'s in East Lancashire and a member of the council of the British Red Cross Society in London.

On visiting the Star and Garter Home for disabled servicemen at Richmond with Sir Frederic Treves during the 1914-18 war, Sir William was so impressed that he formed the Totally Disabled Soldiers Homes at Broughton House and Southport, thereby enabling those living in the North to be near their friends when admitted to the Home. In 1924 he formed the Barrowmore Tuberculosis Colony near Chester for ex-servicemen.

Sir William was in command of R.A.M.C. troops at the Coronations of King Edward VII and King George V and was present in Westminster Abbey at the Coronation of King George VI. He was invited to attend similarly on the occasion of the Coronation of Her Majesty, The Queen, but was prevented by illness from doing so.

An interesting item is that some 70 years ago Sir William received a long and interesting letter from Florence Nightingale concerning the training of men and women in connection with the nursing services. The letter is now in the possession of the British Red Cross Society in London.

As a young man Sir William was very fond of hunting and used to catch a very early train from Manchester to the place where he kept his horse in Yorkshire. Later, on coming to Whalley Range, he kept horses and carriages for his professional work and frequently rode before breakfast, Whalley Range being on the edge of the countryside in those days. He was always a man who anticipated events and needs and, with much regret, changed to a motor car in the earlier days of that method of transport. At one time he was in the habit of bicycling (fixed wheel) 40 miles to join his family for short periods, which enabled him to continue his professional work while they were on holiday. In spite of his long ties with the City of Manchester, he has always been extremely fond of the country and the wild life of the countryside. He was 40 years of age before he started fishing but continued the sport then until close on 90. For many years, from about the age of 55 onwards, he was a keen follower of the Border County Otter Hounds and thought nothing of driving 60 or more miles to a meet.

Lady Coates, until her death in 1949, was actively associated with and of the greatest help to Sir William in all his activities. She herself was Vice-President of the Whalley Range Division of the British Red Cross Society.

It is of interest that Sir William Coates continued his professional work and other activities until over 90 years of age. Though now totally blind and much incapacitated, and so unable to go about, he comes downstairs every day. His mind remains active and he takes a keen interest in current affairs and in the fortunes of the many activities with which he has for so long been associated. In this he is much helped by the wireless, and by his Chauffeur Mr J Jackson, who has been with him for nearly 40 years. Mr Jackson reads at length daily from the newspapers and from numerous books on varied subjects, several of which he always has on hand at once.

Sir William has always been a firm believer in the Christian doctrine and is apt to attribute any success to his faith.

Appendix 2 The Eagle

Right is a picture of the Eagle that was, up until recently, worn by members of 207 (Manchester) Field Hospital (Volunteers) on their service / No 2 dress and below is an extract from the original application (dated 1959) for permission to wear the 'Manchester' Eagle by members of 7th (Manchester) General Hospital RAMC TA. The Eagle had only been approved as a new piece of Heraldry for the City of Manchester in 1958 and the description below explains what each part of the badge signifies.

Figure 90 The Manchester Eagle

```
The Official Badge of the City of Manchester.
(Extract from a document issued by the Town Clerks Department
in May 1958 is appended)

"Lastly, the badge.   This is an heraldic bearing quite
distinct from the arms, and it is not necessarily derived
from elements existing in the arms.   It is intended for
decorative purposes where the full arms would be inconvenient,
and also to act as an identificatory emblem representing the
locality of Manchester rather than the City's corporate entity,
in various emblems.   The badge is thus the proper emblem to
be displayed by organisations which desire to mark their local
but not necessarily official connexion with the City of Manchester.
In its corporate capacity, the Corporation is the only entity
which may display the coat of arms itself, as it was abundantly
proved in the Court of Chivalry in 1954.
The Manchester badge is a golden eagle perched on a white mural
crown, with a red letter "M" inside a red circle on its breast.
The eagle, derived from its prototype on the Roman standards,
represents the Roman origins of Manchester and, with the ring,
its importance as an airport; the white crown stands for the
Cotton Metropolis and the pioneer of "Clean air", and the "M"
figure suggesting the City's name is derived from the arms of
the Wests, manorial successors to the de Grelleys".
```

Figure 91 Extract from a letter sent by Colonel Robert Ollerenshaw to the War Office 20 Jan 1959 (source WO32/18854, The National Archives)

Appendix 3 List of Unit members who have served on operations since the end of the Second War

These lists have been created from memory since no written records are known to exist. Any omissions are purely unintentional.

OPERATION GRANBY (Gulf War 1) 1990-1991

205 General Hospital (Volunteers) Riyadh Saudi Arabia

Lieutenant Colonel Jones

Major Kim Watson (Deputy Matron)

Captain Wendy Marsh

Captain Sheila O'Flagherty

Captain Vic Verengo

Staff Sergeant Linda Atkinson

Sergeant Barbra (Babs) Vinden

Sergeant Ray Woodward

Corporal Andrew (Budgie) Burgess

Corporal Vincent (Vinny) March

Lance Corporal Glen Dwyer

Lance Corporal Patrick (Pat) Farrell

32 Field Hospital

Sergeant Lesley Oldham

Lance Corporal Steele Lloyd

Private Paula Bootham

33 Field Hospital

Sergeant Trevor Heath

Armoured Brigade
Corporal Dominic Connolly
Corporal Barry Curbishly
Germany
Captain Robert (Bob) Jordan
Falklands
Captain Ian Lewin

Northern Ireland
Corporal Andrew Higgins

Balkans
207 Personnel who served in Bosnia, Kosovo and Macedonia
Lieutenant Colonel Cliff Godby
Lieutenant Colonel Steve Laurence
Major Tony Berry
Major Eric Hunter
Sergeant Andrew (Budgie) Burgess
Sergeant Mark Cecil
Sergeant Trevor Heath
Sergeant Aneep Mandviwala
Sergeant Vincent (Vinny) March
Corporal Gaynor Bailey
Corporal Ged Darlington
Corporal Leslie Gandy
Corporal Andrew (Andy) Higgins
Corporal Pamela (Pam) Joy

Corporal Colin McMullen
Corporal David Owen
Corporal James Sadoo
Corporal Jo Tamblyn
Corporal Chris (Traffic) Warden
Lance Corporal Patrick (Pat) Farrell
Lance Corporal Steele Lloyd
Private Darren Smith

EXERCISE SAIF SAREEA

Major Eric Hunter
Major Val Johnson
Captain Sue Evison
Captain Susan (Sue) Flett
Captain Kath Horrocks
Captain Alan Neale
Captain Mark Rowlands
Captain Sharon Stewart
Captain Sally Young

OPERATION TELIC (2003-2009)

Colonel Godby* (Commanding Officer)
Colonel Bhatnagar* (Commanding Officer)
Lieutenant Colonel Mike Godkin* (Regular Second in Command)
Lieutenant Colonel Robin Jackson*
Lieutenant Colonel Steve Laurence
Lieutenant Colonel Thomson

Major Karen Berry*
Major Mary Cardwell
Major David Cook* (Regular Operations Officer)
Major Pauline Dorrington+
Major Colin Gidman*
Major Alison Edwards+
Major Sue Evison*
Major Irene Harrison Bond+
Major Eric Hunter*
Major Val Johnson*
Major Robert (Bob) Jordan* (Quarter Master Technical)
Major Martin Magee* (Regular Quarter Master)
Major Alan McKinnon+
Major Dorothey (Dot) Hibbs Owen+
Major Roger Sharp*
Major Sharon Stewart*
Major Alan Taberner*
Major Paula Tristham* (Regular Nursing Officer)
Major Kerry Trow*
Captain Lynn Anderson+
Captain Satch Atwal*
Captain Helen Ball+*
Captain Phil Broad+
Captain Paul Brown+
Captain Margaret Carr+
Captain Andrew Carrothers+
Captain Patricia Cook*

Captain Simon Davies*
Captain Jerry Diamond
Captain Tracey Elly*
Captain Marion Fleming*
Captain Susan (Sue) Flett+
Captain Wendy Harrison+*
Captain Tony Holland* (Regular Adjutant)
Captain Cath Horrocks+
Captain Stuart Horton* (Regular Adjutant)
Capt Irving+
Capt Johnson+
Captain Malcolm Jackson
Captain Tony Kennie
Captain Linda Marshall*
Captain Ian Miller*
Captain Maia Pelgrom*
Captain Mathew Newton Ede
Captain Angie Nicholls
Captain Derek Robertson+
Captain Rob Rouse*
Captain Andy Tang
Captain Sandie Thorpe*
Captain Sharon Wright*
Captain Sally Young+
Lieutenant Linda Atkinson
Lieutenant Alan Cordwell+
Lieutenant Tracey Heath

Lieutenant Darren Illingworth*
Lieutenant Emma Jinks+
Lieutenant Poole
Lieutenant Anne Shaw+
Lieutenant Sarah Skellon*
Lieutenant Adrienne Unsworth+
Second Lieutenant Paula Gately+
Second Lieutenant Gail Pagent *
Warrant Officer Class 1 (RSM) Pat Hoyte*
Warrant Officer Class 1 Lesley Oldham*
Warrant Officer Class 2 Jonathan Bell+*
Warrant Officer Class 2 Andrew (Budgie) Burgess*
Warrant Officer Class 2 Dominic Connolly*
Warrant Officer Class 2 Stuart Harvey* (Regular RQMS)
Warrant Officer Class 2 Steve Ferguson*
Warrant Officer Class 2 Charles Rowland+
Warrant Officer Class 2 Richard (Ricky) Stock*
Staff Sergeant Rob Brownlow (PSI)
Staff Sergeant Shaun Carter* (PSI)
Staff Sergeant Aneep Mandviwala+*
Staff Sergeant David Morgan+
Sergeant David Bowers (TELIC 2)
Sergeant Trevor Heath+
Sergeant Andrew Higgins*
Sergeant Nigel Hogg+* (PSI)
Sergeant Alison Lloyd*
Sergeant Vincent (Vinny) March*

Sergeant Phil Morgan+
Sergeant David Owen*
Sergeant Gary Woodward+
Corporal Nick Bell*
Corporal Chris Bogart*
Corporal Paul Brook-Stockton
Corporal Garry Cook*
Corporal Ged Darlington+
Corporal Denis Davies*
Corporal Yvonne Flanaghan*
Corporal Colin McMullen+
Corporal Jo Martin+
Corporal Phil Rodgers+
Corporal Murray Tolson*
Lance Corporal Martin Clarey*
Lance Corporal Kyle Eastwood+
Lance Corporal Albert Hicks*
Lance Corporal John (Johnnie) Morris*
Private Hales
Private Hogg*
Private Marshall*
Private Rob Mercer*
Private Lucy Stodart*
Private Paula Waters+

Rear Party for OP TELIC 4

Major Ross Brocklehurst
Captain Chris Carter (QM)
Captain Mary Freeman
Captain Maria May (PSAO)
Captain Alan Bethell (PSAO)
Captain Geoff Hodgson (PSAO)
Captain Mick Thompson (RAO)
Sergeant Ann Hogg
Sergeant Chris Gardner
Corporal Brook-Stockton

* Deployed with 207 in 2004
+ deployed on OP TELIC (often referred to as OP TELIC 1)

Operations in Afghanistan including OPERATION HERRICK (2002-)

Colonel Deepak Bhatnagar*#
Colonel Robin Jackson*# (Commanding Officer)
Lieutenant Colonel Mary Cardwell*#
Lieutenant Colonel Kerry Trow*
Lieutenant Colonel Nick Medway*#
Major Tony Badh
Major Helen Ball*
Major Simon Davies*#
Major Clare Davies-Griffith*
Major Pauline Dorrington*

Major Ray Gregson

Major Eddy Hardaker* (Regular Second in Command)

Major Wendy Harrison*#

Major Steve Hawes*

Major John Hewitt* (arrived back end of tour and continue on to OP HERRICK 13B)

Major Kath Higgins*

Major Angie Nicholls*

Major Rosalind (Ros) Peel*

Major Maia Pelgrom*

Major Nicky Rice*

Major Charles Rowland*#

Major Martin Smith#

Major Sharon Stewart*

Major Neil Sutcliffe

Major Linda Taberner*

Major Jill Winters*
(Joined 207 before joining the Regular Army in 2003)

Padre Banbury

Padre Ian Hall*

Captain Jonathan Bell*#

Captain Beth Hall-Thompson

Captain Tracy Heath

Captain Tim Holland

Captain Michael Hughes*

Captain Annette Lilley

Captain Janet Mills*

Captain Alan Moore

Captain Lesley Oldham*
Captain Jill Rutherford-Davis*
Captain Katherine Wright*
Warrant Officer Class 1 (RSM) Scott Ferris*#
Warrant Officer Class 2 (RQMS) Kevin Duffy (Regular)
Warrant Officer Class 2 Aneep Mandviwala*
Staff Sergeant Jenny Clark (PSI)*#
Staff Sergeant Andrew Higgins*
Staff Sergeant Paul Melia* (PSI)*#
Staff Sergeant Colin McMullen*
Staff Sergeant Julie Misell*
Staff Sergeant Matt Spruce (PSI)
Sergeant Andrew (Andy) Gadsby*#
Sergeant Harold (H) Griffiths*
Sergeant Michael Hawrylkin
Sergeant Kevin Plant (Deployed at same time as 207 attached to 16 Medical Regiment)
Sergeant Phil Rodgers*
Corporal Jo Boorman
Corporal Steve Booth*
Corporal Gary Cook#
Corporal Yvonne Flanagan*
Corporal Scott Jibson (Regular RSI)*#
Corporal Dean Martin
Corporal Lawrence Pleszak*#
Corporal Maxine Simpson*#
Lance Corporal Helen Archer*
Lance Corporal Campbell*

Lance Corporal Paul Corcoran
Lance Corporal Phil Keogh*
Lance Corporal Paul Mattison*
Lance Corporal David Sykes*#
Private Chrissie Barwick*
Private Phil Pullen*
Craftsman Antony Heaford

Rear party for OP HERRICK 13
Lieutenant Colonel Eric Hunter
Major Mike Thompson (RAO)
Major Eileen (Mary) Nixon
Captain Alan Bethell (PSAO)
Captain Alan Fortuin (PSAO)
Captain Geoff Hodgson (PSAO)
Captain Oliver Morris (Adj)
Captain Kevin Thornley (ROSO)
Staff Sergeant John Cave
Sergeant Steve Randeall

* Deployed with 207 in 2010
# Deployed more than once

Often forgotten but without who's help and support no unit can function

Civilian Support Staff
Ms Christine Boggart
Mrs Barbara Boon
Ms Lesley Craddock
Ms Laura Embleton
Mrs Iris Essex
Ms Yvonne Flanagan
Mr Harry Hawksworth
Mr Albert Hicks
Mr Jason Hindley
Ms Laura Horner
Ms Erica Mills
Mr Wayne Moore
Mr Peter Murrell
Ms Sharon (Hope) Nelson
Ms Sharon Potter
Ms Noelle Rigby
Ms Denise Scott
Mr Luke Shepard
Mr Richard Winstanley
Mr Mike Vose
Doreen - from Stores
and Anita, Dylis and Pat

Appendix 4 Annual camps of the Manchester Medical units

Volunteer Medical Staff Corps

    1887   No Annual camp

    1888   Aldershot

Camps from 1889 until the formation of the Territorial Force were held at Aldershot or Netley. During this time one camp was held at Lytham

East Lancashire Field Ambulances

Between 1908 and 1914 camps were held in Lancashire, the Isle of Man, Salisbury Plain and Garstang

    1910   Salisbury Plain

    1939   Four Lane Ends, Lancaster

7th (Manchester) General Hospital

    1965   Penhale, Devon

207 (Manchester) General Hospital

    1967   Catterick

    1968   Aldershot

    1969   Ballybuddon

    1970   Rinteln, West Germany

    1971   Aldershot Church Crookham

    1972   Gareloch Head

    1973   Olen Belgium

    1974   Aldershot Church Crookham

1975 St Martins Plain Folkstone
1976 Olen Belgium
1977 Gosport, Devon
1978 Ripon
1979 Olen Belgium
1980 Longmoor Hants
1981 St Martin Plain Folkstone 1 Week Westdown Salisbury Plain HOSPEX week 2
1982 Liebenau West Germany
1983 Proteus Notts
1984 Tenby
1985 Munster, Germany
1986 Browndown Portsmouth
1987 Saighton Camp, Chester
1988 Lincoln Barracks, Munster, Germany
1989 Westdown Salisbury Plain
1990 Saighton Camp, Chester
1991 Browndown Camp
1992 Crowborough

207 (Manchester) Field Hospital

1993	Westdown
1994	Saighton Camp Chester and Kinmel Park
1995	Crowborough
1996	Saighton Camp, Chester
1997	Gibraltar / Ascension Islands / Edinburgh
1998	Fremington
1999	Redford Cavalry Barracks, Edinburgh and York
2000	RIAT Cottesmore and Fremington
2001	Inverness and Gibraltar
2002	RIAT Fairford / Halton Lancashire
2003	Op Verity Strensall York (pre deployment training)
2004	Rear Party - Redford Cavalry Barracks, Edinburgh with 208 Field Hospital
2005	Penhale Devon
2006	Galloway and Gairlochead, Scotland
2007	Strensall York
2008	Strensall York
2009	St Martin in the Plain, Kent
2010	Strensall, York (support to those personnel deploying on OP HERRICK 13A)
2011	St Mawgan Cornwall
2012	Sennelager, Germany

Appendix 5 Additional pictures

During the course of collecting information for this book we were given hundreds of photographs. It was difficult to choose what to put in and what to leave out. Here are a few that didn't quite make it in.

We have so many pictures that it was suggested we set up a website site in order to share our common history. We would also like to gather stories that you may have of your time with the Manchester Medics. We have registered a domain name manchestermedics.org.uk, why not pop along and visit us.

Detachments

Ashton

Bury

Lancaster

On Exercise

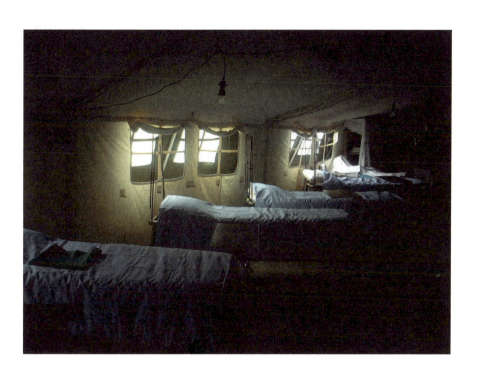

On Ops

Remembrance

The Chefs

The Formal

The Informal

The Exhibitionists

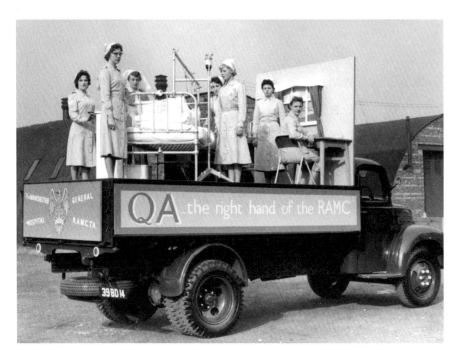

The Training and Challenges

Bibliography

Primary source records not directly referenced in the text

The National Archive

1901 Census of England and Wales

1911 Census of England and Wales

British Army WW1 medal roll 1914-1920

British Army WW1 service records 1914-1920

British Army WW1 pension records 1914-1920

UK medical register 1859-1959

http://www.awm.gov.au/research/people/wounded_and_missing

Secondary sources not directly referenced in the text

Letters received from the Royal Army Medical Corps Military Historical Society

http://www.cwgc.org

http://www.burnleyinthegreatwar.info

http://www.1914-1918.net

http://www.stockport1914-1918.co.uk

References

1. Carver, *The Boer War*. 2000, London: Pan Books.
2. Haldane, R.B., *A speech delivered in Parliament, 8th March 1906*, in *Army Reform and other addresses*. 1907, T Fisher Unwin: London. p. 4-93.
3. Searle, G.R., *A New England? Peace and war 1886 -1918* 2005, Oxford: Oxford University Press. p. 316, 317.
4. Haldane, R.B., *A speech Delivered in Parliament, 25th February 1907*, in *Army Reform and other addresses*. 1907, T Fisher Unwin: London. p. 94-155.
5. Dennis, P., *The Territorial Army 1906 - 1940*. Royal Historical Society studies in history series. 1987, Woodbridge: The Boydell Press.
6. Coates, W., *The evolution of the Medical Services of the 42nd (East Lancashire) Division.* Journal of the Royal Army Medical Corps, 1935. **LXV**: p. 270-279, 334-347.
7. *The Honourable Artillery Company* [Website] July 2008; Available from: http://www.hac.org.uk/html/about-the-hac/hac-history/.
8. Lane, J., *A Social History of Medicine: Health, Healing and Disease in England, 1750-1950*. 2001, London and New York: Routledge.
9. Ponting, C., *The Crimean War The Truth Behind the Myth*. 2005, London: Pimlico.
10. Evatt, G., *The Organization of the Army Medical Services in War Time.* The Nursing Record & Hospital World, 1894. **12** (April): p. 219-221.
11. *Army Medical Services Museum.* [website] September 2008; Available from: http://www.ams-museum.org.uk/historyRAMC.htm.
12. Cantlie, N., *A History of the Army Medical Department*. Vol. 2. 1974, Edinburgh: Churchill Livingstone.
13. Cantlie, N. and G. Seaver, *Sir James Cantlie, a romance in Medicine*. 1939, London: William Clowes and sons Ltd.
14. Gray, P., *Grangethorpe Hospital Rusholme 1917-1929.* Transactions of the Lancashire and Cheshire Antiquarian Society, 1975. **78**: p. 51-64.

15. Smith, J.W., *Six months with a Military Hospital in South Africa.* The Medical Chronicle, 1901. **4**(4): p. 241-267.
16. Brockbank, W., *The History of Nursing at the M.R.I. 1752-1929.* 1970, Manchester: Manchester University Press.
17. Francis, A.E.F., *History of 2/3rd East Lancashire Field Ambulance.* 1931, Salford: W.F. Jackson & Sons, The Manor Press.
18. Simkins, P., *Kitchener's Army The Raising of the new Armies 1914 - 1916.* 2007, Barnsley: Pen & Sword Military.
19. Gibbon, F.P., *The 42nd (East Lancashire) Division 1914 -1915* Military Histories. 1920: Country Life.
20. Stirling, J., *The Territorial Divisions.* 1990, Newport, Wales: Ray Westlake Military Books.
21. *1911 Census of England and Wales.* 2009, The National Archive.
22. Mitchell, T.J. and G.M. Smith, *Medical services casualties and medical statistics of the Great War.* History of the Great War. 1997, London: The Imperial War Museum.
23. The National Archive, *WO374 War Office: Officers' Services, First World War, personal files*
24. Otter, D. and A. Mackay, *Burnley & The Royal Edward Disaster.*
25. Wise, J.E. and S. Baron, *Soldiers lost at sea: a chronicle of troopship disasters.* 2004, Annapolis: Naval Institute Press.
26. Hartley, J. *More than a name.* [Website] 2009 April 2009; Available from: http://www.stockport1914-1918.co.uk/.
27. Thorburn, W., *The 2nd Western Gerneral Hospital.* The British Journal of Surgery, 1914. **2**(7): p. 491-505.
28. Cartmell, H., *For remembrance: An account of some fateful years.* 1919: G. Toulmin & Son Ltd.
29. Light, S. *Scarletfinders.* August 2009; Available from: http://www.scarletfinders.co.uk.
30. The National Archive, *WO95/1603 18 Field Ambulance 1914 Aug. - 1919 Sept.*
31. The National Archive, *WO95/2652 1/2 East Lancashire Field Ambulance 1917 Mar. - 1919 Feb.*
32. Dennis, P., *The Territorial Army in Aid of the Civil Power in Britain 1919 - 1926.* Journal of Contemporary History, 1981. **16**: p. 705-24.

33. Dunbabin, J.P.D., *British Rearmament in the 1930s: A Chronology and Review.* The Historical Journal, 1975. **18**(3): p. 587-609.
34. Dunlop, J.K., *The Territorial Army Today.* 1939: Morrison and Gibbs Ltd.
35. Elder, W., *A short history 207 (Manchester) General Hospital RAMC (V).* Unknown, Manchester.
36. Bradley, H.J., *Heroism of the Hospitals,* in *Our Blitz: Red sky over Manchester.* Unknown, Kemsley Newspapers Limited: Manchester.
37. War Office, *R.A.M.C. training, 1935.* 1939, Army: London.
38. McLaughlin, R., *The Royal Army Medical Corps.* 1972: Leo Cooper Ltd.
39. Otway, T.B.H., *The Second World War 1939-1945: Army Airborne Forces.* 1990, London: Imperial War Museum
40. Carver, *Britains Army in the 20th Century.* 1998, London: Pan Books in association with The Imperial War Museum.
41. Hansard. *House of Commons debates, oral questions and debates, Monday 18th May 1998, Defence, Territorial Army, Column 668.* [Website] 1998 8 April 2010; Available from: http://www.publications.parliament.uk/pa/cm199798/cmhansrd/vo980518/debtext/80518-25.htm#80518-25_spnew9.
42. Guiou, N.M., *Blood transfusion in a field ambulance.* British Medical Journal, 1918. **1**: p. 695-696.
43. Nichol, J., Rennell, T., *Medic.* 2009, London: Penguin Books Ltd.